YEE-HAW! It's

VIZ THE ONE-STRING BANJO

THE FINGER-PICKIN' BEST BITS FROM ISSUES 132-141

Foreword by Abdul Latif
Lord of Harpole and Honorary Duke of Hazzard

" I read 'VIZ'. I am 50yrs. When I grow up my dream is to be an adviser.

Men will come from: Saudi "I have 9 wives and they want me to have 4-5 more wives, Israel and Palestine" we are fighting, how can we stop", John Prescott "how can I have peace?"

My advice to them: read 'Viz' even when sleeping. If this doesn't work try the Lord's World hottest curry, www.curryhell.com

If any animal need advise email me: rentalord@rupali.fsnet.co.uk

SQUEALING LIKE PIGS: Graham Dury, Davey Jones and Simon Thorp. **REAL PURDY MOUTHS:** Alex Collier, Simon Donald, Simon Ecob, John Fardell, Barney Farmer, Robin Halstead, Jason Hazeley, Lee Healey, Angus McKie, Alex Morris, Joel Morris, Paul Palmer, Danny Sanderson, Lew Stringer, Cat Sullivan, Biscuit Tin, Nick Tolson, Brian Walker and Max Yancey. **FASTENING UP HIS DUNGAREES:** Will Watt. **DESIGN:** Wayne 'Boss' Gamble. **WOMEN'S THINGS:** Stevie 'Daisy Duke' Glover.

PUBLISHED BY Dennis Publishing Ltd, The Stoop, 30 Cleveland Street, Alabammy W1T 4JD

ISBN 0-7522-2611-0 FIRST PRINTING Autumn 2006

...D, HE HAD A ...ND HE ENDED ...E. MIND, HE ...O AND ALL SO ...THE FRONT ...E, SO HE ...AMOUFLAGE ...T HE NEVER ...HIDING UNDER ...HIS SISTER'S ...BED IN ...LEICESTER...

20 MINUTES LATER...

...WELL, IT'S ALL INDIANS NOW, YOU KNOW. YOU CAN'T MOVE FOR CURRY SHOPS. NOW, I'VE GOT NOTHING AGAIN' 'EM, I JUST DON'T THINK IT'S RIGHT. I MEAN, HOW WOULD THEY LIKE IT IF WE WENT OVER TO INDIA AND TOOK THE RUDDY PLACE OVER, EH? NO. WELL THERE YOU GO, THIS IS IT, ISN'T IT. AND THERE'S ANOTHER THING...

CAN WE GET ON NOW, PLEASE?

INDEED, YOUR HONOUR.

...MRS. BRADY, PLEASE PLACE YOUR HAND ON THE BIBLE AND READ THE WORDS ON THE CARD...

READ? EEH. I WISH YOU'D TOLD ME, I'D HAVE BRANG ME READERS.

...BUT HAVEN'T YOU JUST FETCHED THEM?

OOH, NO. THESE ARE ME LOOKERS.

MRS. BRADY- COULD ...U JUST TELL THE ...URT IN YOUR OWN WORDS WHAT ...APPENED ON THE ...TERNOON YOU ...RE ATTACKED.

ATTACKED, YES. WELL, I WAS JUST COMING OUT THE SPAR, YOU SEE, BECAUSE I'D GONE IN THERE FOR ME CATFOOD.

CATFOOD, MRS. BRADY?

...AND HE'S ALREADY RUINED TWO CARPETS, THE DIRTY BUGGER, A PATTERNED BERBER AND A TUFTED WILTON AND I WOULDN'T MIND ONLY I WERE STILL PAYING FOR IT.

MRS. BRADY...

...AND DOLLY, SHE SAYS IF Y'RUB BICARB AND NUTMEG INTO THE PILE, SHE SAYS, IT GETS RID OF THE SMELL...

...BUT SHE OUGHT TO PRACTISE WHAT SHE PREACHES, YOU SEE, BECAUSE SHE'S GOT 14 CATS AND EEEH! HER HOUSE, WELL IT BRINGS TEARS TO YOUR EYES...

MRS. BRADY. THIS COURT'S TIME IS VALUABLE...

TEARS!

...SO IF YOU COULD CONFINE YOUR COMMENTS TO WHAT HAPPENED ON THE AFTERNOON YOU WERE ATTACKED...

...YES, WELL I KNOW IT'S TWO BUSES, BUT ...'S THE ONLY PLACE AS DOES CAT-O-MEAT ...ND HE'LL ONLY EAT THEIR DUCK & HEART. ...F HE GETS OWT ELSE HE STARTS SPRAYING.

...S I ALLUS GO TO THE TOP ...NK ON A THURSDAY WITH ...SSIE, YOU SEE, BECAUSE ...EY'VE A GOOD CALLER. A ...OD CALLER HE IS, NICE ...ND CLEAR.

...AND HE'S SMUTTY, ALLUS GIVING THE YOUNG 'UNS AT THE FRONT THE EYE. AND HE JEWED ME OUT ME WINNINGS ONCE BECAUSE I HAD THREE CORNERS AND I WAS WAITING FOR TWO LITTLE DUCKS.

...BUT HE ARGUED THE TOSS. HE SAID MAGGIE'S DEN HADN'T COME UP YET ONLY IT HAD, BECAUSE CISSIE WAS WITH ME AND SHE'D GOT THE CUNTING THING MARKED OFF AND ALL...

MRS. BRADY...

...WOULD YOU RECOGNISE THE MAN WHO ATTACKED YOU IF YOU SAW HIM AGAIN?

OOH, AYE. I'D KNOW HIM ANYWHERE...

...NOT LIKE THAT RUM SO-AND- ...O AT THE MECCA. HE MUMBLES, ...E DOES, SO YOU CAN'T HEAR ...HE NUMBERS. CISSIE SAYS HE'S ...GOT A HARE LIP.

...WELL HE CALLED IT, SO I SHOUTED OUT 'HOUSE'!

I'LL NEVER FORGET THAT FACE, YOUR WORSHIP... NEVER!

COURT WILL RISE FOR THE CASE OF CROWN VERSUS BRADY...!

ADA FLORENCE AGNES PANKHURST BRADY, YOU ARE CHARGED THAT ON JUNE 14th, YOU DID ENTER THE BARNTON ROAD SPAR CONVENIENCE STORE AND THERE DID STEAL A TIN OF DUCK & HEART VARIETY CAT-O- MEAT...

EEH! YOU CHEEKY TURK I'VE NEVER EVEN BEEN TO THE SPAR, IT'S TWO BUSES, YOU KNOW, PLUS I DON'T LIKE THE BUGGER WHAT RUNS IT. TOO FRIENDLY, HE IS, IF YOU ASK ME...

HOW DO YOU PLEAD?

...AND HE'S GOT A FUNNY EYE.

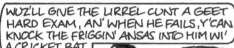

Letterbocks

Bashing the Bishop

According to Bill Bryson in his book *'A Short History of Nearly Everything'*, the vigorousness of a man's beard growth is proportional to the number of times he thinks about sex. This being the case, Archbishop of Canterbury Dr Rowan Williams ought to be ashamed of himself. Filthy beast.

Mrs Yeoman Kidderminster

Although everyone is pleased that rugby hero Jonny Wilkinson escaped uninjured from his recent car smash, in some ways it is sad that Jonny did not die. Being tragically taken from us at the very peak of his career, he would have been remembered as the Buddy Holly of sport. As it is, all we have to look forward to is watching the years take their toll on his once proud physique and his gradual decline into old age.

P Illingworth Staines

Cash Point

Every time I use my local NatWest cashpoint, the screen says 'You have not been charged for this transaction'. Yet when I check my statement, I find without fail that I have had ten pounds debited for every tenner I withdraw. No wonder the banks are raking it in.

Gary Beergut e-mail

Letterbocks
Viz Comic
P.O.Box 1PT
Newcastle NE99 1PT

In this space age you can electromail your letters and tips to letters@viz.co.uk

Judging by all the trophies in his window, our local cobbler/keycutter must be the best in the business.

Craig Greenhill e-mail

Menthol Case

It is a well known fact that koala bears live exclusively on eucalyptus leaves. Bearing this in mind, it follows that their farts should be extremely fragrant. I would like to ask one of *Viz*'s Australian readers to go into the outback, find a koala bear and sniff its arse to see whether its flatulent emissions smell like Hall's Mentholyptus or a Vick's inhaler.

Andy Quinn Huddersfield

Did any of your other readers splutter and chortle when, on Thursday morning's Radio 4 Today programme they interviewed the chairperson of an anti-war group who was called Lindsey GERMAN. The irony.

Steve Denby

Credit Where It's Due

I didn't think it was possible for Ocean Finance to find an uglier set of people to appear in their new adverts than the last lot, but somehow they've done it. Well done Ocean Finance.

WE Barnes Clitheroe

Fragrant Garland

I just farted the first two notes of *'Somewhere Over the Rainbow'*. Does anyone know if they are doing *Pop Idol* again next year?

Andy Muir e-mail

Hot Topic

It's all very well banning the use of mobile phones whilst driving, but what about other hand held objects? The other day, I was driving my car whilst drinking a cup of coffee. As I went round a

---

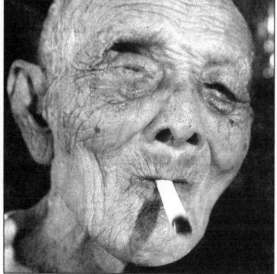
Ab-Fab star in Peg-Leg Rumour Scare

THE WORLD of showbiz was rocked last night as uncorroborated rumours began circulating that one of Joanna Lumley's legs may have been amputated. Details were sketchy, but unsubstantiated suggestions that the *Avengers* star had possibly lost her left leg above the knee were greeted with horror by celebrity insiders.

Fears for the popular actress's wellbeing were further fuelled by groundless speculations that the limb had been surgically removed as a result of thrombosis perhaps caused by the glamorous star's years of possible heavy smoking.

Joanna

"If this is true, then it would be a terrible blow for Joanna," said former *New Avengers* colleague Patrick Macnee. "But if Joanna has indeed undergone amputation, I would imagine that she would be in good spirits after surgery at the Portland Clinic. I dare say she already might be sitting up in bed, laughing and joking with the nursing staff," he hazarded "She's a fighter, and I'm sure she would almost certainly bounce back from a putative tragedy such as this."

Meanwhile Lumley's agent Cunnilingus O'Hara was remaining tight-lipped and refused to be drawn on his client's condition. "There is absolutely no truth in these rumours," he told reporters. "She's with me now, there's nothing wrong with her legs and she's got two of them," he added, further fuelling speculation that Lumley had indeed possibly lost a leg.

sharp bend I spilt some of the hot drink, scalding myself and crashing into three parked cars. This time it was only property that was damaged, but next time I could plough into a bus queue. Come on, Mr Blair. It's time to turn you attention closer to home and outlaw this dangerous practice before I kill someone.

Darren Hyatt
Weston-super-Mare

My mate once told me that if you crash your car into the back of a jam sandwich the guns in the boot go off.

Michael Browne
Leamington Spa

They say that life begins at forty. What bollocks. A mate of mine died in 1983. Last week would have been his fortieth birthday and there's still no sign of him.

Chris Hart
Gotham

Never mind ventriloquists like Keith Harris and Roger DeCourcey. What about Pofessor Stephen Hawking? I saw him on telly blathering on about galaxies for hours and I never saw his lips move once. Genius.

Mike Woods
e-mail

The cost of a stamp in your country would be a lot less if the Post Office spent less money on personalised number plates for its staff, like Pat 1.

John Clarke
Australia

I was shocked to realise I was drinking more alcohol than recommended in Department of Health guidelines. I decided I ought to do something about it, so I quickly drew up my own set of guidelines and I am now well within the recommended level of intake.

D Haslam
e-mail

The government says that there are nearly 50,000 people with HIV in Britain, a third of whom do not even know that they have it. Is it just me, or is it a bit harsh that the government know and haven't told the poor sods?

John Campbell
e-mail

Balloonacy

I was shocked to hear Home Secretary David Blunkett say that Britain's prison population has been ballooning for the past ten years. My God, has the world gone mad? Those people are there to be punished, not to be given 'thrill of a lifetime' experiences that most law abiding citizens can only dream of.

Mrs Close
Headingley

Bring Black's Bling Back!

SINCE the recent burglary on the home of *Cilla Black*, Letterbocks has been inundated with lorras and lorras of messages of sympathy and support for her. Many readers wrote in to share their experiences, whilst others got in touch to ask if there was anything they could do to help. Here's a selection from our postbag.

Headline news ~ Cilla's theft

...My 76-year-old mother was recently burgled and the thieves made off with her wedding ring. Even though it was only worth £100 she was absolutely devastated. Cilla lost £1million of jewellery in her raid, so she must be 10,000 times more devastated than my mother. My heart bleeds for her.

Edna Pentium, Thirsk

...I'm a pensioner who has been burgled four times in the past two days, so I understand what Cilla's going through. I know it's not much, but please find enclosed my £10 winter fuel allowance to buy Cilla some more diamonds.

Ada Tragic, Salford

..My heart goes out to Cilla, but where was her late husband Bobby when she needed him most? Any decent late husband would have scared the robbers off by rattling some chains or coming through a wall with his head under his arm.

Dr U. Foxglove, Rhyll

...Surprise surprise. The cold-hearted insurance company has refused to give Cilla the £1million she needs to replace her treasure simply because she had no window locks in her giant mansion. Surely after all the hours of entertainment this wonderful lady has brought us, the least they could do is pay up. I understand premiums across the country would have to increase as a result, but it would only be a few extra pounds on each policy. It would be a small price to pay to see Cilla dripping diamonds at celebrity parties again.

Bill Kandahar, Stroud

...How many police man-hours are spent each year chasing murderers, rapists and paedophiles? And yet the evil monsters who broke into Cilla's house and stole her jewels seem to have got away scot free. Isn't it time she got a fair crack of the whip? I suggest the government sets up a special 100,000 strong police force to be called the CID (Cilla Investigation Department) to hunt these men down and cage them once and for all.

Zelda Bond, York

...I live in a remote African village. Everyone here was really upset to hear about Cilla's diamonds getting stolen. We have sold our cattle, some chickens and a plough to raise some money for her. It's not much, but it will be worth it just to see her bedecked in gaudy jewels again.

Pipi Okwekwe, Africa

...Cilla has always been the Queen of theSaturday night TV schedules. Since she has lost her jewellery it would be a lovely gesture if Queen Elizabeth were to make her a gift of the Crown Jewels currently kept in the Tower of London. They may be slightly less ostentatious than the ones that were stolen, but I'm sure she'd get used to them.

Mrs Pendleton, Pendoggett

TOP TIPS

LECTURERS. Clear nail varnish makes ideal tippex for correcting mistakes on overhead transparencies.
P A Hallows
Manchester

MOTORISTS. Avoid getting prosecuted for using your phone whilst driving. Simply pop your mobile inside a large shell and the police will think you are listening to the sea.
A Corten
Caerleon

SINGLE men. Convince people that you have a girlfriend by standing outside Etam with several bags of shopping, looking at your watch and occassionally glancing inside.
Tubbs
e-mail

DURING winter, put Pop Tarts on your radiators so you can have a warm snack throughout the day whilst saving electricity on your toaster.
Dave Oxendale
York

SHOES last twice as long if only worn every other day.
Clare Hobley (34E)
Manchester

JEREMY Beadle. When selling DVDs on yout TV advert, hold the discs in your bigger hand so that they do not appear to be the size of laser discs.
Gladdy
Airdrie

WHEN replying to Nigerian lawyers that offer millions in return for a £50,000 finders fee, only send half the money. Keep the rest until you get the paperwork.
Dr Maldwin Palmer
e-mail

READERS. Don't waste money buying a copy of *Bridget Jones' Diary*. Simply dig out your twenty year-old copy of *The Diary of Adrian Mole* and cross out all the references to 'spots, replacing them with 'fat arse'.
Chris Cowen
e-mail

BIRD lovers. Save money on wild bird food this winter by fitting a bird feeder to the inside of your window. You only need to fill it once, but you will enjoy watching the birds at your window every day!
Lee Nelson
Stockton-on-Tees

IMPOTENT men. Don't waste money on expensive drugs like Viagra off the internet. Just let your wife think you don't fancy her.
A Davis
e-mail

4X4 DRIVERS. Use your bull bars as a handy mobile railing on which you can tie flowers in memory of the people you run down.
M Trouserman
Birmingham

toptips@viz.co.uk

GILBERT RATCHET

HER MAJESTY THE QUEEN IS COMING TO FULCHESTER TODAY, TO DECLARE OUR NEW LORD MAYOR OFFICIALLY OPEN

FULCHESTER WELCOMES HER

AND HERE COMES THE ROYAL COACH - HUZZAH!

I'M AFRAID THE MAYOR-OPENING CEREMONY WILL HAVE TO BE POSTPONED AS THE QUEEN CAN'T COME OUT OF HER CARRIAGE

GOSH! BUT WHY?

HER MAJESTY DELIBERATELY ROED HER KNICKERS FOR A JOKE ~ BUT NOW WE CAN'T GET HER CLEANED UP BECAUSE THE ROYAL MUDFLAP POLISHER PURSUIVANT HAS SPRAINED HIS WIPING ARM

HE IS THE ONLY PERSON PERMITTED TO ATTEND TO THE REGAL BUMCRACK.

NOT TO WORRY

I'LL INVENT A REMOTE-CONTROLLED "WIPE-O-MATIC" WHICH WILL ENABLE US TO CLEAN UP THE QUEEN'S BOTTOM WITHOUT ACTUALLY TOUCHING IT.

SEE ~ THE ROBOT AUTOMATICALLY FOLLOWS THE HAND MOVEMENTS I MAKE IN THESE SPECIAL COMPUTERISED GLOVES

HOW INGENIOUS!

A BIT MORE TO THE LEFT, GILBERT ~ THERE'S A WINNIT AT 3 O'CLOCK

WIPE WIPE

NOW START RUBBING GENTLY UP AND DOWN THE CLEFT

THEN - WOW! A WASP!

SWIPE FLAIL

GET AWAY FROM ME, YOU PEST!

STOP WAVING YOUR ARMS AROUND, YOU IDIOT! YOU'RE FLINGING THE QUEEN'S POO ALL OVER THE SHOP!

OOPS!

OH CRIKEY! THE LORD MAYOR HAS COPPED A FACEFULL

SPLAT!

GASP! YOU'RE IN BIG TROUBLE NOW, GILBERT

THROWING THE MONARCH'S FAECES AT A LORD MAYOR CONSTITUTES HIGH TREASON ~ AND IS PUNISHABLE BY DEATH!

OO-ER

GO AHEAD, EXECUTIONER

WHAT THE -?! THIS ISN'T GILBERT AT ALL

THUNK

SPARK ZAP

IT'S MERELY A HOME-MADE ROBOT REPLICA

MEANWHILE AT GILBERT'S HOUSE

I COULDN'T BE BOTHERED TO GET OUT OF BED THIS MORNING, READERS

SO I INVENTED THAT "GOING-THROUGH-THE-MOTIONS-O-MATIC" ROBOT REPLICA OF MYSELF TO TAKE PART IN THIS CARTOON FOR ME.

Test YOUR Circus Funnyman Knowledge~ YOU are the Clown

You are standing on one side of the ring when your colleague drives in in a small car. Suddenly, the doors fall off and a lot of white smoke comes from under the bonnet. He approaches and asks you to look under the bonnet. What do you do?

Answer ~ You should refuse to do as requested several times. Eventually, you give in to your colleague's request, lift the bonnet and press the hidden button that squirts the water out of the radiator into your face.

Half way through the second half of a show you are on a stepladder sticking wallpaper onto a wooden partition wall in the centre of the ring. Suddenly, the ringmaster appears and tells you very publicly to leave the ring as you are making too much mess. How do you respond?

Answer ~ The correct course of action is to come down from the ladder with the paste bucket and chase the ringmaster several times around the ring. Wait for him to stop and duck before throwing the bucketful of confetti over the audience.

You find yourself sitting in your dressing room with a stinking hangover when you suddenly realise that you are 60- years old, have no money put by, and are living in a series of muddy fields. It also dawns on you that nobody actually enjoys watching your show, and that you merely fill in time whilst the good acts prepare their equipment. What do you do?

Answer ~ In this situation you should down another bottle of Netto own brand whisky before putting your head in the CalorGas oven in your caravan.

HUGH HEFNER WAKES AFTER 51 YEAR DREAM

EXCLUSIVE!
By our Jazz Correspondent
Ralph Malph

HUGH HEFNER, the multi-millionaire publisher of *Playboy* magazine, awoke yesterday to discover that the last fifty-one years of his life had all been a simply marvellous dream and he was actually an assistant floor manager in John Menzies.

The no-longer rich and enviable soft-porn magnate awoke to find himself stacking tippex on a low shelf at the back of the Huddersfield branch of the newsagents and stationers. Witnesses reported that after blinking a couple of times and shaking his head, he sighed deeply and went to answer a staff call for a price check on Memorex C90s at the back till.

DREAM

Later, as he rolled a cigarette on his lap in the staff tea room, Hefner told colleagues that he'd "had the most wonderful dream".

"He explained that he'd been living in an enormous mansion, surrounded by nude women with breasts the size of their heads," Darren Bannock, trainee till operator at the branch, told us. "He looked quite sad to find out that none of it was real and that he actually only earns £5.25 an hour and rents Janine's box room.

FISH

Customers noticed a tear rolling down the only-rich-in-his-head shop manager as he cut the plastic straps round a bundle of Men Only to put on the top shelf next to where, had his 51-year-long dream actually been true, face-out copies of his own legendary grumble mag would have been proudly displayed. But instead of the entirely imaginary *Playboy* magazine that Hefner fantasised had made his fortune, there was merely a gap and a note reminding him that it was "Time to order more *Parade!*".

Psychologists forecast that the no-longer-enviable now-father-of-none will return to his real life, with only his impossibly magical memories to comfort him as he grinds through the remaining years of a futile life where no six foot blondes queue up to drape their arms round him, just like the rest of us.

THE BED

"When he put his coat on and helped lock up," Shelly Manford, the shop's Duty Manager told reporters, "he kept looking at me, disappointedly. He said that, if he hadn't woken up, I'd have been 20 years younger and screwing him in a Jacuzzi by now. It's tragic, really."

Hugh, (left) ~ can only dream of the empire he once dreamed he built, and (above) some of the magazines that never existed that didn't build it.

An artist's impression of Hugh's dream

PISTOL LYDON IN WITH A BULLET!

FOUL-MOUTHED King of the Jungle *JOHN LYDON*, aka loveable Sex Pistol Johnny Rotten, last night added another crown to his crown collection when he was crowned Crown King of Comedy! Readers of *TV Quick* magazine voted his ostrich-fighting performance in this year's *I'm a Celebrity Get Me Out of Here* the funniest thing ever on television, even beating favourites such as Basil Fawlty, Del Boy and Compo going down a hill in a bath.

Here's that chart in full:

TV's Top 10 Funniest Moments...

1 *JOHNNY ROTTEN* fighting live ostriches while covered in molasses and birdseed – now officially the funniest thing that has ever happened

2 *BASIL FAWLTY* goose-stepping out of the front door of *Fawlty Towers* with a dead German under his arm

3 *THE FAT ONE FROM THE OFFICE* dressed up as Mr T wanking into the photocopier tray

4 *CAPT MAINWARING*'s classic 'Don't mention the war, Pike!' in the Hitler's Testicle episode of *Dad's Army*

5 *DELBOY* falling into Grandad's grave dressed as Batman and Robin

6 *RICKY TOMLINSON'S ARSE* in the puppet version of *The Royle Family* wallpapering Caroline Aherne's husband, the late Peter Cook

7 *BLAZIN' SQUAD* being asked the same question 22 times by Jeremy Paxman on *University Challenge*

8 *KENNETH WOLSTENHOLME* rushing onto the pitch shouting 'I think it's all over' in the closing minutes of the 1966 world cup final and scoring a goal

9 *VICTOR MELDREW* answers the phone with Mrs Slocombe's pussy, and says 'I don't believe it!' in *One Foot in the Grave*

10 *SID JAMES* pulling Barbara Windsor's tits off and eating them in 70s sitcom *Sid & Nancy*

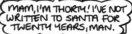

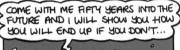

...mind the DOORS

★ ★ ★ ★ ★ ★ ★ ★ ★ ★ ★ ★ ★ ★ ★ ★ ★ ★

• I grew up in a house with doors in it, and it's left me with a lifelong love of them. Now I have a house of my own, and I have a door in every room. Some rooms have even got two.

J Barnestaple, Rhyll

• When I was a boy, my parents' house had two doors, which they referred to as the 'front door' and the 'back door'. Whilst the front door was indeed at the front of the house, the so called back door was actually down an alley at the side. I remember once someone delivering a new fridge to our house. *'Could you take it round to the back door?'* my mother cheerily asked. The poor man walked straight past it! It still makes me laugh today.

T Couts, Glamorgan

• *'Get yourself an education - it opens so many doors'* my father would always tell me when I was little. Of course, I didn't listen to him, and dropped out of school when I was 15. The funny thing was, I got a job straight away... *as the doorman at a local hotel!* I've been there for thirty five years and opened more doors than I care to remember. So I had the last laugh.

J Pritchett, Bude

• I own a small shop on the outskirts of Leeds. One morning as I opened my shop, the door fell off. It appeared that woodworms had eaten into it and weakened the timber around the hinges. But I didn't have to go far to get a new door... it's a door shop that I own, and I simply bought one off myself.

F McNally, Leeds

• As a boy, I always loved the door to my grandfather's house. It was a deep red colour and had the most beautiful stained glass in it. *'I'll leave it to you in my will'*, he often told me. I thought he was joking, but he was as good as his word. When he died, he left instructions to the executors of his will to remove the door and take it round to my house. It was a very emotional moment- when I fitted it in place at the front of my house. My grandmother was furious, however. Without a front door, some burglars marched straight in and cleaned her out whilst she slept.

M McCloud, Birmingham

• Shakin' Stevens may have had a hit with the song 'Green Door', but he didn't have one in his house. I'm a painter and decorater in Cardiff, and I did his front door last week... *duck egg blue!*

Norbet Golightly, Cardiff

• I've always been a great fan of kitchen doors, especially the ones that swing in two directions. The other day, I was delighted to see a Laurel and Hardy film on TV where the pair get a job in a hotel kitchen, and I settled back to enjoy the doors. My delight soon turned to anger. Not two minutes into the film, the fat one, carrying a large stack of plates was sent flying, plates and all, by the thin one opening the door *the wrong way!* They were sacked by the little man with the moustache and the kitchen doors did not feature any further. My blood boiled. Had they followed the accepted catering industry proceedure of walking through the right hand door, the accident would not have happened and a perfectly enjoyable film would not have been ruined.

Alfred Biggles, Chester

• The other day, I went shopping as I do each and every Wednesday morning at 9.00 o'clock, rain or shine. When I got back at 11.00, I realised I had left my front door key at the bakers shop in town. Fortunately, I keep a spare key hanging on a piece of string behind the letterbox for just such emergencies.

Dorris Rabbit, 32 Oakenfield Avenue, Barnchester

• *'As one door closes, another one opens'*, my father once said when I was little. However, he remedied the situation by putting spring loaded stays on top of each door and draft excluders along the bottom.

J Geils, Folkston

• I went to buy a new front door from a builders merchant last week. I selected one at a cost of £48. The man in the store asked me if I would like a letterbox cut out of it and I accepted. Imagine my horror when he charged me £2 for cutting the hole. Correct me if I'm wrong, but a door with a letterbox has less wood than a door without one, so it should be cheaper, not more expensive. No wonder door manufacturers all drive around in Rolls Royces.

Hector Dunwoody, Leigh

• A couple of months ago I put a new front door on my house. The following day, my neighbour put a new front door on his. A week later I painted mine blue and he followed suit. Yesterday, I put a doorbell on it, and guess what?... he put a door bell on his. I put the number 36 on mine this morning. I dare say tomorrow there'll be a 36 on his door.

P Harper, Harpenden

Kids say the Funniest things... about doors!

..My grandson looked at the house number on my front door the other week. 'Do those numbers let people know how old you are, gran?' he asked. I wouldn't have minded, but I live at 324 Acacia Avenue. I don't look that old!

Edith Barnett, York

...'Look, mummy, that door's broken. It's got all holes in it', my daughter once said in the kitchen. She was pointing at a louvre door!

Margaret Barnes, Stoke

...'Granny! Granny! Why don't cars have their numbers on

their doors like houses do?' my grandson asked me the other day. I wouldn't mind, but he's 36 years old.

Ada Sykes, Hull

...'Could you answer the door?' I called to my grandson when the bell rang. 'I don't know, gran', he replied. 'What did it ask?' I've never liked him, the sarcastic little cunt.

Joan Timeshare, Totnes

Miriam

ANSWERS YOUR DOOR PROBLEMS

Dear Miriam... | **LETTER OF THE DAY**

I live in a small, very friendly street where everyone knows everyone else.

I am 54 and my neighbour is 51 and we have always been great friends. Recently, however, he has been calling the entrance to his walled garden the 'side door'. Granted it is six foot high and made of wood, but as the bricks do not go over the top of it, surely it is a gate, not a door.

I don't want to fall out with him over something so petty, but I don't know how much longer I can go on listening to him refer to this gate as a door.

AR, Bolton

Miriam says... This is something you need to sort out now before it ruins a perfectly good friendship. For what it's worth, I was always taught that if you could hold a bargepole aloft and carry it through, it was a gate. But your neighbour may have been taught differently.

Have you spoken to him about it? He may have a special reason for calling it a door. Or he may be perfectly happy calling it a gate if you tell him how it's upsetting you. You may just have to agree to differ and hope your relationship is strong enough to get you through the disagreement.

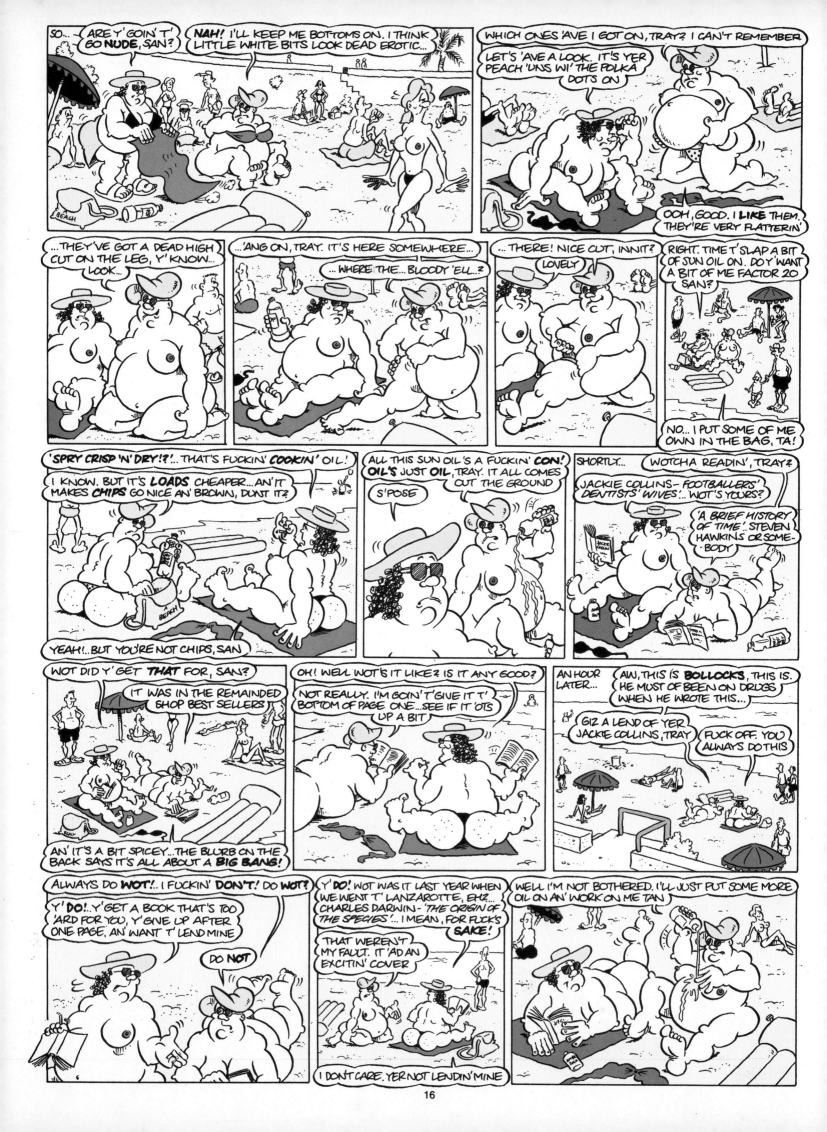

NONCE PROBLEM

EXCLUSIVE!

SOLVED!

A RADICAL new proposal to deal with Britain's convicted sex offenders is causing uproar in communities affected by the change.

Currently, people on the Sex Offenders Register are either kept in prison where they can be safely killed by fellow inmates or released into the community to have dogshit pushed through their letterbox and their houses burnt down while they are battered to death by cab drivers. But fears about the safety and effectiveness of these two options have led government boffins to seek new ways of dealing with the problem.

cross

"Nobody wants a paedophile or a rapist living next door," consultant Crimonologist Dr Timothy Toothpaste told us. "It makes people antsy and cross. But we have to deal with these undesirables somehow. Kiddie fiddlers and aggressive

High paed rail ~ British Nuclear Fuel's train to take nonces to the sea (left) and a BNFL technician who checks on safety (right)

cottagers are like nuclear waste. We want to hide them away and forget about them, but no-one wants them disposed of in their backyard. That's why we decided to go to the experts, BNFL."

krishna

British Nuclear Fuels Ltd say that the commission from the Home Office came as a surprise, but they are convinced they can rise to the challenge.

"We have years of experience in handling dangerous things that the public would rather pretend didn't exist. It's just a matter of switching from radioactive fissile and waste material, to men with milkbottle glasses who live with their mothers."

redknapp

BNFL estimate that they will be able to transport up to four thousand gallons of nonces a day by rail in secure containers direct from the courtroom to processing stations on

Atomic Boffins to Pump Diddlers into Sea

the world's coast where they will be pumped into the sea.

kiri

But residents of towns along the rail route are furious about the proposals.

"What happens if the driver of the train gets some egg sandwich in his eye and drives the engine into a signal box?" complained campaigner Cramphorn Campayne at a champagne reception to launch the residents' protest.

"If that happens, the train will turn over and spill dangerous sex-pests and Jonathan Kings all over the embankment. Anyone playing near the railway will be at risk from having their bottom touched or being invited to see puppies. Accidents will happen. And it's our children who'll suffer."

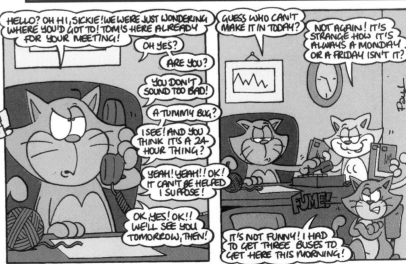

the GIFTS of the MAGI

IT AIN'T 'ALF A LOAD OF OLD SHITE, MUM!

Forces morale lowest ever as Star Quality hits rock bottom

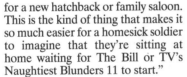

Fucking rubbish ~ The galaxy of stars that failed to shine at the Combined Forces' Show. Clockwise from the top - Howard Halifax, the Yes Car Bird, AOL's cyberbint Connie, and Douglas, the Plasticine Lurpak butterman. Meanwhile, right - The Golden Olden days of Forces entertainment, Windsor Davies and Melvyn Bragg.

OUR BRAVE armed forces in Iraq are reportedly on the verge of rebellion against superior officers following a bargain basement effort to keep them entertained.

Army morale is said to be at an all-time low following a variety show held at a secret desert location just outside Baghdad last month. The show featured such household names as Howard from the Halifax commercials, AOL internet girl Connie, the blonde girl in the green body warmer from the Yes Car Credit advert, and Douglas the little man made out of Lurpak butter.

cream

But organisers have responded angrily to the suggestion that the line-up for the not very lavish display of the cream of British talent was simply a case of opportunistic product placement.

penetration

"We're only too aware that over the past year our troops have been starved of access to celebrities of this calibre," explained Bombadier Hector Lewerthwaite, spokesman for the Gulf Combined Forces' Entertainments Committee.

"The four performers we chose to front the gala evening are hugely popular back home right now. We had Connie from AOL talking about the benefits of parental control and a speedy broadband connection immediately after the Yes Car lady had explained about easy fixed rate loans

By Our Defence Correspondent, a pre-heart transplant
Eddie Large

for a new hatchback or family saloon. This is the kind of thing that makes it so much easier for a homesick soldier to imagine that they're sitting at home waiting for The Bill or TV's Naughtiest Blunders 11 to start."

or drop

Failing to raise a laugh, or even a flicker of recognition from the entertainment-hungry crowd, the branded foursome broke into an impromptu and humiliating dance routine before aggrieved squaddies voted with their mouths and stormed the stage, finally using a struggling Douglas to butter some army-issue scones.

"It's simply not good enough," complained Private Tommy Atkins of the Durham Light Infantry, currently stationed in Basra. "In the Second World War, forces' entertainment was provided by big names like Bob Hope and Dame Vera Lynn. There was proper talent on display. Even that prize cunt Jim Davidson they got in the Falklands would be preferable to this lot."

trouble

Troops were even more angry after hearing rumours that American forces were being treated to live sex shows with Tiger Woods getting gobbled off by Buffy the Vampire Slayer while Justin Timberlake let her have it through the back door.

Meanwhile, Defence Secretary Geoff Hoon has responded to the

forces' complaints by requisitioning international roly-poly singyman Rik Waller and hideous looking Nora Batty actress Kathy Staff.

"They will be flown out to Iraq next week where they will keep the troops happy with a display of lion taming, ice dance and party cake decoration," a spokesman for the Ministry of Defence said.

Latifebocks

STAR LETTER

I SEE on the news that Lord Hutton says he is "satisfied that David Kelly took his own life". He may not have liked Dr Kelly that much, but isn't this taking gloating just a little too far?

Dave Owen, Edinburgh

They say that if you lay down with dogs, you get up with fleas. Well I laid down with a right dog after a beach party in Magaluf last summer, and fleas would have been a fucking blessing compared to what I got up with.

M. Earcat Bargoed

Top marks to the humorous sub on the *Brighton & Hove Argus* who managed to slip this headline past his eagle-eyed editor.

Robert Johnston Brighton

My mate told me that his pitbull terrier's bark was worse than its bite. Well, after plastic surgery and 132 stitches to the back of my leg, I am dreading hearing it bark, I can tell you.

Christopher Hampshire Bristol

I am a lorry driver and I am proud to say that I haven't killed any women now for over 20 years. Perhaps your readers will finally see that we're not all bad after all.

Garry Beergut Barton Park Services

Letterbocks
Viz Comic
P.O. Box 1PT
Newcastle NE99 1PT

In this space age you can electromail your letters and tips to **letters@viz.co.uk**

Getting out of my car the other day at my local sports centre, I received an angry glare and verbal abuse from a disabled driver as I had parked in a disabled space. I apologised and moved my car, parking ten yards away in a normal parking space.

Later, I saw the same man in a wheelchair, training on the athletics track for a 10km race. I find it ironic that he wouldn't travel the extra 10 yards from the normal parking spaces, but would happily sit pushing himself round an oval track for two hours. Once again, it is one law for the disabled and another for everyone else.

R Murphy Liverpool

In amongst some old wank mags I was chucking out, I recently found an old copy of *Viz* in which you referred to the Queen Mum as a 'coffin dodger'. I bet you feel foolish now.

Mike Spiers e-mail

After suffering a head-on car crash in Northumbria recently, who should I see rubber-necking slowly past the wreckage but haughty TV chef Clarissa Dickson-Wright in her Volvo. Did she stop to offer assistance? Did she bollocks. When she inevitably croaks from heart disease, I fully intend to dance on her grave.

G Bryant, Sheffield

I have recently been very bored and as a result ended up re-reading some old issues of *Viz*. In number 108, Billy the Fish was drawn in amazing 3-D graphics, and Tommy Brown promised us a look at "...the shading on Brown Fox's tits." Now I know what you are thinking, just because I haven't had sex since May. I've turned into the kind of sad, pathetic individual who masturbates over Lara Croft (which I haven't, ever), but it's not that. I am just a keen fan of 3-D computer art and I am really interested. From an artistic point of view. So come on, *Viz*, let's have a look at those tits.

Nugget e-mail

* *Yes, Mr Nugget. Here you go.*

The recent suicide of Harold Shipman has thrown up some interesting questions. For a start, does Shipman killing himself take his official tally up to 216, or does it count as an own goal? Where does this final score place our national champ in the world league table?

Magnus, Sheffield

If Predator can only see hot things through his thermal imaging eyesight, why doesn't he fall over twigs and branches when he's hunting Arnie in the jungle? I realise I should have asked this question fifteen years ago, but I've only just rented the video.

Catian Redring Glasgow

I saw an advert for Oil of Ulay that said it could make anyone look ten years younger. Rubbish. I put some on my nine year-old daughter and it didn't make her look minus one.

Mike Mirkin, e-mail

People who are up in arms about Samantha Marson, the girl who joked that she had bombs in her bag at Miami airport, are missing the main point - the joke simply wasn't funny. For goodness sake, if you are going to risk being locked up for a couple of weeks, at least do a decent knob gag, or one about the mentally handicapped.

Lord Schmoo, Bicester

Returning to the office after a business meeting the other day, my colleague said "I have an important doctor's appointment this afternoon, you'll have to drive like the wind." I had to laugh, sine the wind speed that day was 5mph, and it

WE'VE GOT THIS LICKED: Susan Howlett with 16st Cromwell who got trapped in mud after slipping into a lake and had to be rescued by two passers-by

Ring sting

Thieves stole my

A JEWELLER had £250,000 worth of diamond rings stolen in an elaborate sting.
Adam Alexander, who is constantly aware of...

"I still can't believe it. I can't believe no one saw anything" Mr Alexander is convinced it was a set-up.
Police believe the jeweller was tar...

TOP TIPS

CAR thieves. Don't be discouraged when nothing is on view. All the valuables may be hidden in the glove box or under a seat.

Tim, e-mail

PETER Andre. Don't make a fool of yourself trying to have sex with Jordan in the jungle. Simply become a professional footballer and wait your turn.

Tim, e-mail

IF YOU see curly-headed funnyman Alan Davis in the street, DON'T take his photograph as he recently told reporters that it really annoys him.

Rhiannon Collier Newcastle

BAKERS. Avoid confusion and imprisonment when carrying desserts through airport customs by referring to Almond and Mocha bombs as Almond and Mocha upside-down cakes.

M Kipling, Guantanamo Bay

LEEDS United. Help yourself out of debt by not picking up the Ticket Line phone, and then putting it down again when your supervisor whispers to you to do so.

Angry Matt, Goole

HAVE fun in the supermarket next time you go alcohol shopping. Fill you trolley to bursting point with booze, then add one packet of nappies. When paying, pretend that you don't have enough money and put the nappies back. Watch the faces of the checkout personnel. Priceless.

Wax, Addlestone

SAVE money on expensive surround sound home cinema systems by only watching films when the appropriate noises are going on outside, eg watch horror movies when there is a storm on, or cowboy films whilst local drug gangs are fighting it out in the street.

Andy Mansh, Cheltenham

WORM farmers. Double your yield by simply cutting every worm in half. Hey presto! Each half will grow into a new worm.

Laurie, France

DEPRESSED people. Instead of attempting suicide as a 'cry for help', simply shout 'Help!' thus saving money on paracetamol, etc.

Stephen McGrath, e-mail

SAVE HOURS in every working day by hanging the clock upside down at 10.05am. That way, it's 4.35pm and only 25 minutes to home time.

Sod Robin, Leicester

was blowing in a south easterly direction, the opposite way to the office. Needless to say my colleague missed his doctor's appointment.

Ian Krender, Ascot

This Value Added Tax is a rip-off. I was expecting a great deal on a car the other day, and I ended up having to pay an extra 17.5% for it. There is no way that's added value. If anything, I'm about three grand out of pocket.

Jon Cooke, Leicester

Can any Viz-reading lawyers tell me it is legally acceptable to sell naked pictures of myself as a child to peedos? Me and my missus were at my parents' the other week when the old photo albums were brought out. Whilst trying to ignore the giggling and pointing at my under developed genitals, I realised that I could be sitting on a little goldmine.

C Dawson, London

What's happened to the Queen Mother these days? She never seems to be on the telly anymore.

T Allchin, Sevenoaks

Thought For the Day with Max Yancey

Have you ever wondered why ants always seem to be in a hurry? They are always busily going to and fro and never seem to achieve anything or pause for breath.

When I was younger I had an ant farm in my room. It was fun to make their tunnels collapse or put half the tank under water and to see the ants struggle for their lives.

Finally, they were doing something productive, something that mattered: They were entertaining me.

Looking back on that now, I can't help but wonder if my actions were those of a sensitive human being. Childhood memories are like looking into a whirlpool of emotions, aren't they? So many happy moments, tinged with sadness, wrapped in a cloak of mystery.

I love children, but not in the wrong way. So that's great. I'm Max Yancey. Do you know who **you** are?

The Doctor will C of E you now

YOUR medical problems with the Archbishop of Canterbury Dr Rowan Williams

Flu jab gives me needle

Dear Doctor,

I am 83 and I was wondering whether or not to have a flu jab this winter. I don't really like injections and, as I have lived a righteous life, surely God would not strike me down with flu.

Edna Golightly, Arsenal

Dr Williams replies,

• I'm afraid it's not as simple as it may first appear. The Lord has power over large things, such as earthquakes, lightning, amphibious plagues, etc. Unfortunately, flu is caused by a virus which is very small and God is from before there were microscopes. So he may find it difficult to prevent the transmission of air-borne diseases. In these circumstances, it may be better to have the jab.

★★★★★★★★★★★★★★★★

A Tadger Unfair

Dear Doctor,

I am 53 and I have been diagnosed with prostate cancer, despite having been a chaste churchgoer all my life. I read a recent report which said that this cancer is less prevalent in men who masturbate regularly from an early age. It seems rather unfair that God should put people such as Cliff Richard and the Pope at risk, whilst the likes of Peter Stringfellow and Martin Clunes are rewarded with some measure of protection from this disease.

Harold Hadrada, Pately Bridge

Dr Williams replies,

• Yes, on the face of it, it may seem unfair, but just consider how much richer your life has been because you have never touched yourself under the bridge. You may be taken twenty years before your time, but the Lord will bless you with life everlasting, whereas the fornicators and onanists will live a long life full of carnal pleasures, but face an eternity of agony and suffering. So it's swings and roundabouts really.

PROBLEM of the WEEK

Dear Doctor,

After being hit on the head by falling masonry in our local church, my husband has spent the last six months in a coma. He is being fed via a tube, but I am concerned that, due to his condition, he is unable to say grace. Will this cause him a problem at the Pearly Gates if he doesn't pull through, or would the grace he said before breakfast on the day he was injured still be valid? Should I ask the medical staff to stop feeding him anyway, just to be on the safe side?

Mrs Corbett, Crouch End

Dear Doctor,

I'm a dustman, and I've had a bad back off and on for the past three years. My old doctor signed me off whenever it played up. Now I have a new doctor who says I'm swinging the lead and refuses to put me on the panel. I can't stay off without a sicknote, or they'll dock my pay. Could you get an angel or something to visit my boss in a dream and tell him whenever I'm unfit for work?

Mr Donegan, Cumberland

Dr Williams replies,

• Fifty-eight million work hours per year are lost due to bad backs. A period of bedrest is often the only thing that works. Yes of course I will ask, and I'm sure the Lord will send a cherubim or seraphim to intercede on your behalf. But remember, God is omnipresent and sees everything - if he spots you mowing the lawn or doing a bit of decorating while you're on the sick, then he'll come down on you like a ton of bricks.

★★★★★★★★★★★★★★★★

Leg us Pray

Dear Doctor,

On a recent trip to Ghana, my 8-year-old son contracted Necrotising Ebola.

Dr Williams replies,

Any grace said is valid for one meal only - a bit like buying a salad at Pizza Hut entitles you to one trip to the salad bar. So I'm afraid your husband is definitely not covered by the grace he said on the morning of his tragic accident. However, God judges every case on its own merits, and it may be that on judgement day he will take into account your husband's persistent vegetative state.

As for stopping his feeding regime, I'm afraid only you can make that decision. But before making up your mind, just consider - every time nutrients are about to be inserted into his feeding tube, and he fails to thank the Almighty for what he is about to receive, your husband commits an abomination in His eyes. And great will be the wrath of the Lord and swift and mighty shall be His vengeance.

It is a particularly aggressive infection, and it's working its way up his leg. The doctors say they can stop it with powerful antibiotics, but I believe that using medicines is interfering with God's will, and I have decided to pray for him instead. How should I do it?

Dinsdale Trelawny, Raith

Dr Williams replies,

• I agree that medicines are interfering with the Lord's plan. If he had wanted us to use antibiotics, he would have made them grow on trees to be picked like apples. I recommend that you pray for your son three times a day after meals. But you must do it properly with your eyes shut. If he doesn't get any better in a few days, you may need to try a more powerful prayer and shut your eyes even tighter.

Do They Know it's Christmas?

It was the Supergroup to end all Supergroups. A glittering line up of Rock Royalty. Everyone who was anyone in the world of music, and Bananarama, turned up at Sarm Studios that day in 1985, and the rest is history.

The intervening years have been a rock and rollercoaster for many of the stars featured on the single. But after two decades and with the holiday season fast approaching, are the Band Aid stars still aware of what time of year it is? We called them up to ask… *Do They Know it's Christmas?*

Boneo, *U2*

"Yes, I know it's Christmas, but I don't celebrate it anymore because I've gone Jewish. Or possibly Buddhist. It's that one where you put red string round your wrist. Like Madonna and David Beckham have done. So I've had to give up Christmas because it's against the rules. But I'm still going to do Easter because I love chocolate eggs."

George Michael, *Wham*

"Of course I know it's Christmas. It's my favourite time of the year and the only time I get a break from my extensive recording and touring commitments. I usually have a very traditional Christmas surrounded by family and friends. We all get up early to open our presents, then everyone settles down for a traditional lunch of turkey and all the trimmings. We'll watch a film in the afternoon and then have turkey sandwiches for tea. Later on in the evening I might pop to a public lavatory to masturbate at a policeman."

Tony Hadley, *Spandau Ballet*

"Do I know it's Christmas? You betcha! It's the busiest time of the year for me. I spend all day playing Santa Claus in the grotto at our local garden centre. It may seem an unusual career move, but I think I had taken my music as far as I could and I wanted to explore new avenues. And at night I stack the freezers at Iceland in Smethwick."

Sting, *The Police*

"I hate the tacky commercialisation of Christmas which seems to start earlier every year. My wife Trudi and I long for a simple Christmas, one in tune with its humble beginnings and true meaning. So we've bought an island off the coast of Mustique and evicted all its inhabitants so as we can enjoy this special time undisturbed."

Rick Parfitt, *Status Quo*

"I know it's Christmas, but it doesn't mean a lot to me these days, to be honest. I had a heart transplant some years back and there was a bit of a mix up. To cut a long story short, I ended up with the heart out of Schnorbitz, Bernie Winters's dog. Now I have seven Christmases a year and the sparkle has gone."

Boy George, *Culture Club*

"No I don't know it's Christmas, and I don't even know what Christmas is. During my well-publicised period of excessive drug use, the bit of my brain that recognises religious festivals was burnt out by some bad acid. As a result, I not only don't know it's Christmas, I've no idea if it's Easter, Yom Kippur or Divali either. Coincidentally, another part of my brain was irreparably damaged at the same time, the bit that enables one to identify stupid hats."

Phil Collins, *Genesis*

"Christmas? Is it really? I had no idea. I live in Switzerland these days and Christmas is very different over here. There is no snow for a start, and the Swiss don't have a Christmas tree in the house, they have an enormous cuckoo clock made of cheese which they cover with tinsel and baubles. And you won't find a sixpence in your plum duff in this country- instead you'll find a bar of nazi gold."

Simon le Bon, *Duran Duran*

"Yes, I know it's Christmas. It's a very busy time of year for teen idols like myself. There are millions of Durannies out there who want to know if our Christmas single will beat that of our arch rivals, the Spands. And they want to know what nutty things me and the lads will get up to behind the scenes at the Top of the Pops Christmas special. I won't tell you what prank we've got up our sleeves, but look out Haircut 100 – you might find your dressing room filled with shaving foam!"

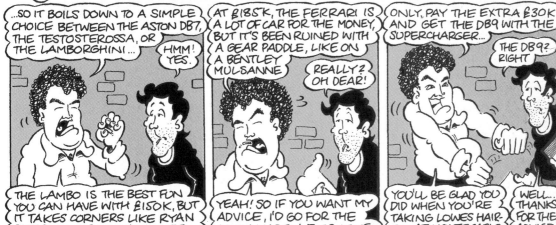

THE ADVENTURES OF **JEREMY CLARKSON** THE PETROLHEAD MOTORMOUTH

Live Longer, Earn More and Have Better Nookie?

HOW'S THAT FOR STARTERS!

FORGET exercise, the Atkins Diet and quitting fags and booze. The key to a long life is having a starter before your main course! That's according to a new report from Oxford University's Department of Hors d'Oevres, Nibbles and Starters.

According to boffins, diners who regularly tuck into appetizers such as garlic bread, prawn cocktails and breaded mushrooms-

● **HAVE** a markedly lower cholesterol level
● **LIVE** twice as long
● **ENJOY** more three-in-a-bed sex romps
● **EARN** four times as much money

as people who go straight for the main course.

Professor **Steve Langton**, who conducted the two-week study, said he was very surprised by the findings. He told us: *"When we processed the data, we saw the results and couldn't believe our eyes. We thought the computer must of blown a fuse, but we checked the plugs and they were all fine. It was a huge thumbs up for starters."*

However, others have been quick to condemn the report. **Richard Anselm** of anti-starter group **STOPSTART** told us: *"Professor Langton's study is a load of nonsense. Nowhere in it does he explain how his reseach was conducted, or how he reached his conclusions. He appears to have simply made it up off the top of his head. The fact that the study was financed by the starter industry speaks for itself."*

But Langton was keen to defend his one and a half page report. He told us: *"The methods used to collect and analyse the data were so complex and involved that I didn't think anyone else would understand them. That is why I didn't bother including them in the final report, and just published the findings on their own in the form of a press release to tabloid newspapers."*

A spokesman for the British Starter Council told us: *"We in the starter business have always known the benefits of having something to put you on while you're waiting for your main course, but to have it scientifically confirmed like this by Professor Langton and his team is very gratifying."* And the timing of the report is also likely to delight starter industry big-wigs, coming as it does just as they launch British Starter Week at venues up and down the country.

With interest in starters expected to boom following the report, eateries are gearing up to meet the unprecedented demand for soups, melon boats and potato skins with sour cream dips. Aggressive chef **Gordon Ramsay** told us: *"When I read the report, I immediately punched and sacked both my main course chefs. Then I hired two new starter chefs. And punched them."*

First course gets top marks ~report

"From now on it's starters only at my restaurant," he added. *"If you ask for a main course or pudding I'll come out of the kitchen and punch you and your wife."*

Your Starters

EVERYONE has a favourite starter, be it soup or something else. We phoned up ten celebrities and asked them "What's your favourite starter?" Unfortunately, six just put the phone down, but four were happy to tell us their top starter.

Roly-poly funnyman **Peter 'Garlic bread?...GARLIC BREAD?...Garlic?...Bread?' Kay**, famous for his catchphrase 'Garlic bread?...GARLIC BREAD?...Garlic?...Bread?' didn't hesitate. "I suppose you'd expect me to say 'Garlic Bread?...GARLIC BREAD?...Garlic?...bread?' But you'd be wrong... because it's soup," he told us. However, fat beer ad king Peter had the last laugh when we asked him what flavour soup he preferred. "Cream of garlic bread," he quipped.

U2 front man **Bonio** was in Cuba addressing the World Health Organisation on the subject of the Kyoto agreement when we caught up with him. "I fly all over the world talking about environmental issues, and wherever I'm eating, I always have the same starter - a simple prawn cocktail." he told us. And there's never any chance of it being off the menu - because each one is made in his favourite Dublin restaurant and flown out in a specially chartered jumbo jet to wherever he is in the world. "Dublin prawns help me remember my roots and keep my feet on the ground," he added.

26

Are YOU a Non-Starter?

Are **YOU** the kind of person that likes a starter before a meal? Or are you the type that prefers to get stuck into the main course? It's often hard to tell. Answer the Questions truthfully to find out once and for all whether you like starters or not.

START

You buy something in a charity shop for £1.50 and pay with a £10 note, but receive change for £20. Do you point out the mistake to the assistant?

Would you tell a lie to get a woman into bed?

An intriguing parcel is delivered to your house in error. Do you take a peek inside?

In the street, would you step into the road to avoid walking under a ladder?

Does the idea of having sex in a public place turn you on?

Your car has been broken into. Do you claim on the insurance for something that wasn't stolen, such as a camera?

You see someone drop a £5 note in the street. Do you pick it up and keep it?

You are on a crowded bus when an old lady gets on. Do you give up your seat for her?

Do you think personality is more important than looks?

You are looking at the menu in a restaurant. Do you order a starter?

Congratulations, you're definitely a starter person. Whether you're sipping soup, gobbling up garlic bread or doing something beginning with 'p' to a prawn cocktail, you don't think a meal's complete without a starter first.

Oh dear, it's no starter for you. Perhaps you're not a big eater or are you saving a bit of space for extra pudding or some cheese and biscuits... maybe even both? Whatever the reason, starters are definitely a non-starter for you.

for Ten

*'I'm a Celebrity... Get me out of here' tit model **Jordan** had a surprise choice. "I suppose you'd expect me to say two large melons with cherries on the top. But you'd be wrong," she told us. "I like nothing more than two large grapefruits with cherries on the top. I'm proud of my breasts and I'm not ashamed to eat starters that resemble them in some way," she said.*

*Grinning 'Changing Rooms' host **Carol Smillie** was slightly less forthcoming about her choice of starter. "Who the fuck is this? Have you any fucking idea what time it is? It's three in the fucking morning," she joked. "How did you get this fucking number? You might think this is funny, I fucking don't. Ring this number again and I'll call the fucking police," she laughed.*

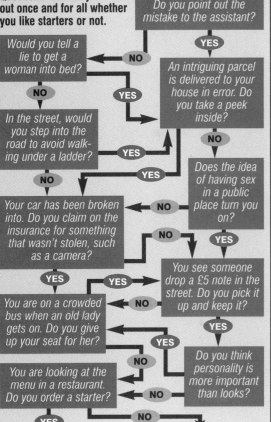

Appetizers, hors d'oeuvres, antipasties. Call them what you will, one thing is certain; starters are here to stay, and that's official. We look for them on menus, we order them before our main meal and we eat them prior to commencing our second course. They're the talk of John O'Groats from Land's End to the length of the land and that's a figure that's set to double. But how much of what we say about them is true? Get your teeth into these...

10 things you never knew about STARTERS

1 Starters are named after *Sir Henry de Montford, 5th Earl of Start* (1536-1602). At a banquet where the food was taking a long time to arrive, he produced a flask of soup which he began to eat. He declared it *"a most efficacious way to commence one's repast"*. In no time at all, the whole of London society had joined the craze and were having fashionable soup 'starters' before their main courses. It was not until a century later that the Duke of Bread Roll (1675-1734) requested a small baked bun to mop up his soup, so setting another trend which continues to this day.

2 In August 1997 a simple prawn cocktail was responsible for robbing the country of its Princess of Hearts. During her final supper at the Paris Ritz, Lady Di uncharacteristically decided not to have a starter. "If she had ordered a first course she would have taken at least 11 minutes longer to finish her meal. So instead of colliding with the white Fiat Uno in the Pont d'Alma tunnel, driver Henri Paul would have missed it by over 8 miles, and tragic Diana would have emerged unhurt at the other end," said an expert.

3 The term *starter* is said to derive from the fact that starters were responsible for 'starting' the English Civil War. Following an Indian meal at a restaurant, a dispute over the bill arose between *Charles I* and *Oliver Cromwell*. The King, who had had an onion bhaji and a rogan josh wanted to split the bill equally. But Cromwell refused as he'd only had a main course. A scuffle ensued which later developed into a 30-year conflict claiming over 600,000 lives.

4 The biggest starter in the world was eaten by Monster Truck driver *Chad Kyminski* during the 1996 Ohio State Fair. He entered a branch of *Pizza Hut* in Dustbowl City and ordered a garlic bread the size of a football field. He consumed the huge slice in 10 minutes, before tucking into his main course, a deep pan meat feast with mushrooms... *12 miles in diameter!*

5 If someone doesn't order enough starters, it is said that he 'under orders starters', but did you know he could also be 'under starters' orders'? This is nothing to do with not ordering enough starters, it means to be under the orders of the starter, the man who fires the gun to start a race.

6 Also, if a swimming teacher tells a group of novice swimmers to dive beneath the surface, it could be said that he 'orders starters under'.

7 The world's smallest man, *Calvin Phillips*, never has a meal without a prawn cocktail starter. But to Action Man-size Calvin, a normal prawn is the size of a lobster! So he tucks into plankton in mayonnaise made from hummingbirds' eggs... *all served up in a glass thimble!*

8 Probably the most famous starter is the Holy Eucharist, a sort of religious garlic bread that the vicar puts in your mouth to keep you going until your main course of the second coming of our Lord Jesus Christ.

9 The eating of starters is not just confined to restaurants. Amazingly, it has also been seen in the natural world. Tigers will often eat a few rabbits to keep them going before tucking into their zebra main course.

10 You might think that a 'twisted fire starter' is a starter which has become twisted in some way and has caught alight. But you'd be wrong, for it's actually a record by pop group the Prodigy. Scary spiky-haired singer Keith Flint got the idea for the song when he was visiting a Berni Inn with his mum and dad. "I ordered a garlic bread, and when it arrived it had been twisted in some way and had caught alight," he told the NME.

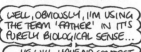

ROGER MELLIE

THE MAN ON THE TELLY

Roger has got a job on Radio One, standing in as guest presenter on the breakfast show

OK ROGER, WE'RE JUST GOING TO RECORD SOME TRAILERS FOR YOUR SHOW NEXT WEEK.

READY WHEN YOU ARE, TOM.

AND, CUE!

Hiii! ROGER MELLIE HERE AND I'VE GOT A SEN-FUCKING-SATIONAL WEEK LINED UP FOR YOU HERE ON RADIO ONE EFF EM...

CUT!

WHAT'S UP, TOM?

THAT WASN'T QUITE RIGHT, WAS IT ROGER? LET'S TAKE IT FROM THE TOP.

WAKE UP EVERY MORNING NEXT WEEK ON THE BREAKFAST SHOW, WHEN I'LL BE SPINNING THE PLATTERS THAT MATTER ~ ALL YOUR FAVOURITE GOLDEN OLDIES!

YES, I'LL BE DUSTING OFF ALL THOSE WRINKLY OLD CUNTS LIKE ROD STEWART AND.. ERM.. WHATSISNAME, THAT GINGER TWAT. FANNY FEATURES OUT OF SIMPLY RED

CUT!

STILL NOT QUITE THERE, IS IT ROGER? TRY AND REMEMBER — THIS IS THE BREAKFAST SHOW ON RADIO ONE

NO SMOKING

ALL RIGHT, LET'S TRY IT ONE MORE TIME.

JOIN ME, ROGER MELLIE, ON MONDAY'S BREAKFAST SHOW WHEN I'LL BE TALKING TO A FANTASTIC GUEST IN THE STUDIO — KYLIE MINOGUE!

AND HEY! I'M NOT NORMALLY A BACKDOOR MAN MYSELF, BUT I'D PARK MY COCK UP HER ARSE ANY DAY OF THE WEEK

CUT!

HOW ABOUT YOU, TOM? WOULD YOU GIVE KYLIE ONE UP THE FARTER?

SILENCE

ROGER, STOP. I'M SORRY. THIS JUST ISN'T WORKING AT ALL...

... YOU'RE GOING TO HAVE TO SWEAR A LOT MORE THAN THAT IF YOU'RE GOING TO BE AS OBNOXIOUS AND UNPLEASANT AS CHRIS MOYLES.

I KNOW. I'M SORRY TOM. I JUST DON'T THINK I'VE GOT IT IN ME.

OH, LORDY, IT'S THE FAT SLAGS

WHAT D'YER THINK OF ME NEW CAR, TRAY? IT'S A CONVERTIBLE.

A CONVERTIBLE?

THE FIRE BRIGADE'S 'AD THAT ROOF OFF, SAN. IT'S BIN IN A SMASH.

I DON'T CARE. I THINK IT'S SMART. ANYWAY, WE'RE OFF TO BAZ'S IN IT. HE'S EXPECTIN' US.

I DIDN'T KNOW YOU 'AD A LICENCE.

OH AYE.

...WELL...IT'S NOT A FULL LICENCE...

PROVISIONAL?

BLOCKBUSTER CARD.

FUCKIN' 'ELL, SAN. YER TAX DISC'S OUT OF DATE AN' ALL! SHALL WE STOP AT POST OFFICE AN' GET A NEW ONE?

NO. YOU NEED AN MOT FOR ONE OF THEM...

...AND INSURANCE.

YER NOT INSURED? WHAT'LL Y'DO IF YER GO INTO THE BACK O'SOMEONE?

SIMPLE. I SEEN IT IN THIS FILM ON THE ADULT CHANNEL.

FIRST THING Y'DO WHEN Y'AVE Y'CRASH IS TAKE YER KNICKERS OFF.

OH AYE?

AYE. THEN, WHEN THEY COME TO Y'WINDOW, YER PULL Y'SKIRT UP, GIVE 'EM A GLIMPSE OF Y'SNATCH AN' OFFER 'EM A "KNOCK F'KNOCK" SETTLEMENT.

A WHAT?

Y'KNOW. A F—

BANG!

PRIVATE

LONDON SYMPHONY ORCHESTRA & FESTIVAL CHORUS ON TOUR

LSO68

GET Y'KNICKERS OFF, SAN. I'LL RING BAZ AN' TELL 'IM WE'RE GOING TO BE LATE.

ME FIRST, THEN THE REST OF THE STRINGS...

... THEN THE HORNS AND WOODWIND... AND THE PERCUSSION SECTION...

33

34

Letterbocks

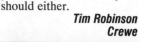
THE TWO PENCIL STAR LETTER

IN Limp Bizkit's new single Fred Durst can be heard singing 'no one knows what it's like to be mistreated'. I feel my pet rabbit would disagree, having recently starved to death in a nest of its own excrement.

Zoot, Aberdeen

* Not one, but TWO Knackersack pencils are on their way Mr (or Mrs) Zoot.

Letterbocks
Viz Comic
P.O.Box 1PT
Newcastle NE99 1PT

In this space age you can electromail your letters and tips to letters@viz.co.uk

I WAS really upset to read in my Sunday paper that Rowan Atkinson was suffering from depression after critics rubbished his James Bond spoof movie *Johnny English*. There are many films far worse, such as *Rat Race* for example. Now that was shite.

P Accrington Stanley

I HEARD a fruit seller shout 'Fuck off shitcunt' at an elderly lady in a London market recently. Isn't it comforting to know that the famous Cockney wit is still with us in these troubled times.

Lang Streak Barnet

HOW come in the adverts, a McDonald's Big Mac looks as tall as one of the twin towers (when it was still standing, of course), yet when you get one they're as squashed as my gran's tits?

Big Mick High Wycomb

ONE day I phoned my son in Australia to have a chat. However, I must have dialled the wrong number, as it was answered by a young lady. I apologised, and we had a little chat. The following day, I phoned the same wrong number and got the young lady again. How we laughed at my silly mistake. That was twenty years ago. Although we have never met, we have become firm friends and I call her every single day. She always loves to hear my news.

Edna Brakespear Burnley

I HAVE just watched '*Nigella Bites*' where she made a mozzerella toastie, and the director went to some lengths to ensure that when

she ate it there were close ups of her mouth with stringy cheese smeared over it. For God's sake, why don't a couple of cameramen do money shots onto her face in the titles so we can get on with the cooking without all this mindless innuendo? You don't see Anthony Worral-Thompson stooping to tactics like shaving his beard like a fanny and then munching on a fat salami.

Mother Truffle e-mail

I AM becoming sick and tired with the media's politically correct obsession with gay sex. It's getting so that I can't turn on the Fantasy Channel without seeing two naked homosexual women indulging in these sordid practices. I'm thinking of cancelling my subscription.

T Cutt Surrey

I HAVE always preferred the radio to television as I believe the pictures in one's imagination are better than one gets on the small screen. So imagine my outrage when I pictured the gay kiss between the chef from Grey Gables and Adam Macey from Home Farm in last week's episode

of *The Archers*. And to broadcast it at 7.30 in the evening when small children could be picturing it was truly irresponsible.

Hector Nottingham Hector

IT'S uncanny how some of these old sayings are true. 'Absence makes the heart grow fonder', said my wife as she waved goodbye to me on the way to spend a month with her mother. Since then I have grown quite fond of my next door neighbour. I actually gave her one on the living room carpet this morning.

Christopher Hampshire Bristol

I SAW a mink yesterday... wearing fur! If the mink population simply cannot be bothered to set an example, I see no reason why we should either.

Tim Robinson Crewe

TIM Robinson (above letter) should not tar all mink with the same brush. I am a mink farmer, and many of my animals have given up wearing fur. In fact they all give it up sooner or later.

G Crampston Suffolk

Stars' Relief as Lumley Monoped Rumours Quashed

THE WORLD of show-biz breathed a sigh of relief late last night as rumours that one of Joanna Lumley's legs had been amputated were scotched. Stories that the veteran *Sapphire and Steel* actress had lost her left leg above the knee had begun circulating in the late afternoon, and were greeted with horror by celebrity insiders.

However, at a hastily-called press conference in London's swanky Grosvenor House, a smiling Lumley sipped a glass of water before standing up in front of reporters to reveal two healthy legs which were clearly complete and real from above the knee to the foot.

"As you can see, both Joanna's legs are in great shape," said her agent Fellatio Nelson. "We don't

know why or how these rumours got started, but we're happy to set the record straight." And he made a plea that the popular actress be left alone to get on with her career.

Meanwhile fellow celebrities were delighted at the announcement. "This is marvellous," former co-star David McCallum told us when we broke the news. "It's been a very worrying few hours for all her former co-stars. We've all been praying for her to have two legs, and it seems as if our prayers have been answered."

SMITH—YOU'RE THE BOTTOM OF THE CLASS.

TOP TIPS

WANKERS. Save yourself much embarrassment by checking that none of your housemates have come home from work sick and are sleeping in their rooms before you put a porn vid on in the living room with the volume on high.

Lachlan Barker
e-mail

WHEN very drunk and taking a shit, never under any circumstances stop to blow your nose when wiping your arse.

Marc Johnson
Leigh-on-sea

IN A RUSH? Cook your breakfast egg in half the time by replacing the water in the pan with commercially available brake fluid which boils at 200˚c.

Carlos
Northern Ireland

A SIMPLE check that your wife has not accidentally left Flash Toilet Wipes on top of the cistern instead of the usual Andrex moist bum wipes will avoid cross words and marital discord.

Paul Berriman
e-mail

PREVENT burglars stealing everything in the house by simply moving everything in the house into your bedroom when you go to bed. In the morning, simply move it all back again.

Anthony Smales
Beverley

FATHERS. If you have a new-born baby, never made a derogatory comment on your wife's skills as a mother.

Marc Johnson
Palace Hotel
Southend-on-Sea

VINYL enthusiasts. Re-create that old fashioned stuck needle sound when listening to an mp3 on your computer by occasionally pressing CTRL+ALT+DEL mid song.

Mike Harbidge
e-mail

DRIVERS. If a car breaks down or stalls in front of you, beep your horn and wave your arms frantically. This should help the car start and send them on their way.

Paul
South Africa

Tinker?...Tailor?...Soldier?...Sailor?... Cyclist?...Scientist?...Egg Farmer?...Tramp?

Oakey Dokey

Win £100 worth of fags in our Human League-tastic 'What's Phil Oakey Doing Now?' competition!

'YOU WERE working as a waitress in a cocktail bar, when I found you.' So sang eighties electro-synth pop maestro **Phil Oakey** out of The Human League. But twenty years on, there's only one question on everyone's lips... *What is Phil doing now?*

The rest of the band's whereabouts are well known: keyboard player **Martyn Ware** left to form Heaven 17 before quitting music to become an astronaut. He was poisoned by a leak of antifreeze on the Mir space platform, and now has a mental age of three. Guitarist **Ian Graig Marsh** similarly announced he had enough of the chart scene in the mid eighties and is now deputy leader of the Transport and General Workers Union. Both of **the girls** stayed in the music industry, except for a brief period when they became waitresses in a cocktail bar. After becoming the two girls in Bucks Fizz, they left to become the girls in Brotherhood of Man. *But what of Phil?*

Here are 8 things that Phil could be doing now... but 7 are made up.
To win the fags, simply tell us which one is TRUE!

Oakey JOKEY?
Phil travels the country working as a clown in Jerry Cottle's Circus. He specialises in filling his trousers with custard, climbing a ladder with wallpaper and driving an exploding car. ①

Oakey CHOKEY?
Convicted in 1992 of aggravated rape, Phil was sentenced to 15 years in prison. He was denied parole in 1998 following a fight in which another inmate was glassed in the eye. ②

Oakey SMOKEY?
Phil sank his record royalties into a tobacconists shop in Rotherham. He now has a chain of 15 throughout S.Yorkshire and sells over £20000 worth of pipes and ciggies each week. ③

Oakey BROKEY?
When the hits stopped, Phil's jetset lifestyle caught up with him and in 1991 he was declared bankrupt. He now lives on a bench in Roundhay Park, Leeds. ④

Oakey SPOKEY?
With time and money to spare, Phil pursued his hobby of cycling. He joined Team Cofidis and competed alongside David Millar in the 2002 Tour de France, finishing a creditable 7th. ⑤

Oakey CROAKEY?
After The Human League, Phil took a degree in Amphibian zoology at Sheffield Hallam University. He is now professor of frogs at top American college Harvard. ⑥

Oakey YOLKEY?
On the death of his uncle, Phil inherited a 50% share in an egg farm. He now has over 6 million chickens and is responsible for 25% of the UK's total egg production ⑦

Oakey STROKEY?
Phil lapsed into a coma after a blood clot from his knee blocked the major artery feeding his brain. He is now in a persistent vegetative state in the Royal Hallamshire Hospital. ⑧

Send your answer, along with your name and address to *'Oakey Dokey Competition, Viz Comic, PO Box 1PT, Newcastle upon Tyne, NE99 1PT'.* The competition is not open to anyone entering unless the fags are for their dad. All entries must be in... The first prize has been donated by the 'Together In Electric Dreams' Tobacconists, High Street, Rotherham

SORRY. COMPETITION CLOSED!

FRU T. BUNN
THE MASTER BAKER & HIS GINGERBREAD SEX DOLLS

OOH, FRUBERT. THERE'S WASHING ON NEXT DOOR'S LINE. THE NEW PEOPLE MUST'VE MOVED IN.

HMM?

...AND FANCY THAT. I THINK HE MUST BE A BAKER TOO, JUDGING BY HIS WASHING.

HMM..?

...AND HE'S MARRIED.

MARRIED? HOW DO YOU KNOW?

WELL HIS WIFE'S SMALLS ARE HANGING ON THE LINE TOO.

SMALLS!?

BINGO! LOOK AT THE SIZE OF THAT PASTRY BRA! ≋SLURP!≋

SHE MUST HAVE MERINGUE TITS LIKE MOCHA AND ALMOND BOMBS!

AND I BET THEM SHORTCRUST SCANTIES HAVE SEEN A BIT OF ACTION...!≋PHWOOOAR!≋

I CAN'T WAIT TO GET A PROPER LOOK AT HER!

ERM... I'M JUST GOING TO THE GARDEN SHED TO... ERM... ER... TO OIL THE...ER... SHEARS.

THAT'S NICE, DEAR.

...BUT WHY ARE YOU TAKING YOUR BINOCULARS WITH YOU?

WHAT? THESE?

ER... ERM...

IT'S IN CASE I CAN'T FIND THE SHEARS AND ERM... ER... THEY'RE FAR AWAY.

BUT SURELY...

SLAM!

5 HOURS LATER...

...I WONDER WHERE FRU'S GOT TO..?

THOSE SHEARS MUST BE RUSTIER THAN I THOUGHT.

GREAT! HE'S GETTING TIRED. HE'S GOT TO BE UP EARLY... THAT'S IT... OOH, YEAH!... OFF TO BED, YOU LOVEBIRDS!

HEH-HEH! THAT'S RIGHT, LEAVE THE BEDROOM CURTAINS OPEN.. PUT ON A GOOD SHOW FOR OLD FRU 'T'...

I WANT TO BE ABLE TO SEE IT GOING IN.

SHIT! SHIT! SHIT! HE'S SHUT THE CURTAINS.

BLOODY HELL FIRE.

AH, FRUBERT. THERE YOU ARE. I'VE KEPT YOUR TEA WARM IN THE OVEN...

NOT NOW. I'M JUST GOING UP TO THE LOFT TO... ERM...

ER...

...TO CHECK THE ROOF JOISTS FOR WOODWORM.

RIGHT! NOW FOR A PROPER HARDCORE GINGERBREAD PEEP-SHOW!

≋DROOL≋

HERE WE GO. RIGHT OVER THEIR BEDROOM.

GENTLY NOW, FRU 'T'..SOFTLY SOFTLY CATCHY SPUNKY...

PHWOOAR! JESUS! HE'S LICKING HER OUT, THE JAMMY BASTARD!

I'M GOING TO HAVE TO VIDEO THIS.

TERRY FUCKWITT

We're on holiday at the seaside, readers. I love playing in the sand.

Look mum! I've buried dad up to his neck! Ha ha!

That's nice, Terry. However, there is one small fly in the ointment...

Eh?

...We're NOT on holiday at the seaside — we are in a cemetery, where we are attending your father's funeral.

You may recall that you killed him a few days ago when you tried to give him a surprise haircut with a power drill.

Sorry mum. Bugger me, I'm a right clot.

Excuse me. Perhaps we could return the late Mr Fuckwitt to his grave and continue with the funeral.

What the hell's going on here?

Dad! You're alive!

And what's this graveyard doing in my living room?

Can't I take an afternoon nap without being involved in some fuckwitted charade?

Terry, you're such a pig-ignorant shit-for-brains that it's started to affect your mother. She's getting all confused. I think we all need a holiday at the seaside.

I–I'm a bit confused myself, dad.

Well, how can I make it clearer for you, son? How can I put it in a way that you are able to understand?

Ah, yes, I think I see a way...

HOOF!

OOYAH!

There, now get your suitcase packed. We're going to the seaside.

Righto dad. I'm with you now.

AT THE SEASIDE

Here, Terry. Take our towels and things and find a nice quiet spot on the beach where we can do a bit of sunbathing.

Even a thick twat like you should be able to manage that.

EVENTUALLY

Ah! Here's a good place to soak up the sun.

Dad! Over here! I've found the perfect spot!

Well it's nice and sandy, certainly. And it's secluded, I'll grant you that.

I would however question the suitability of this location for sunbathing...

You see, Terry, this is the planet PLUTO, which is 3½ thousand million miles from the sun, and has an average temperature of minus 229° centigrade.

Fuck me.

Consequently it is probably the worst place in the entire solar system to do a bit of sunbathing.

Honestly, Terry, you really are a gormless cunt.

BACK TO EARTH

LATER

Dad's right. I'm an absolute arsewit.

ONE POUND

Oh well. I'll cheer myself up with an ice cream.

You don't want an ice cream, Terry. You want to hit this old world war two percussion mine with a sledgehammer.

Erm... I do?

Yes! And it'll only cost you a pound.

That's it, Terry. Give it some welly.

CLANG

KA BOOM!

Fuck me, readers, I haven't got the brains I was born with...

...they're over there, being pecked by that seagull.

40

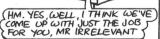

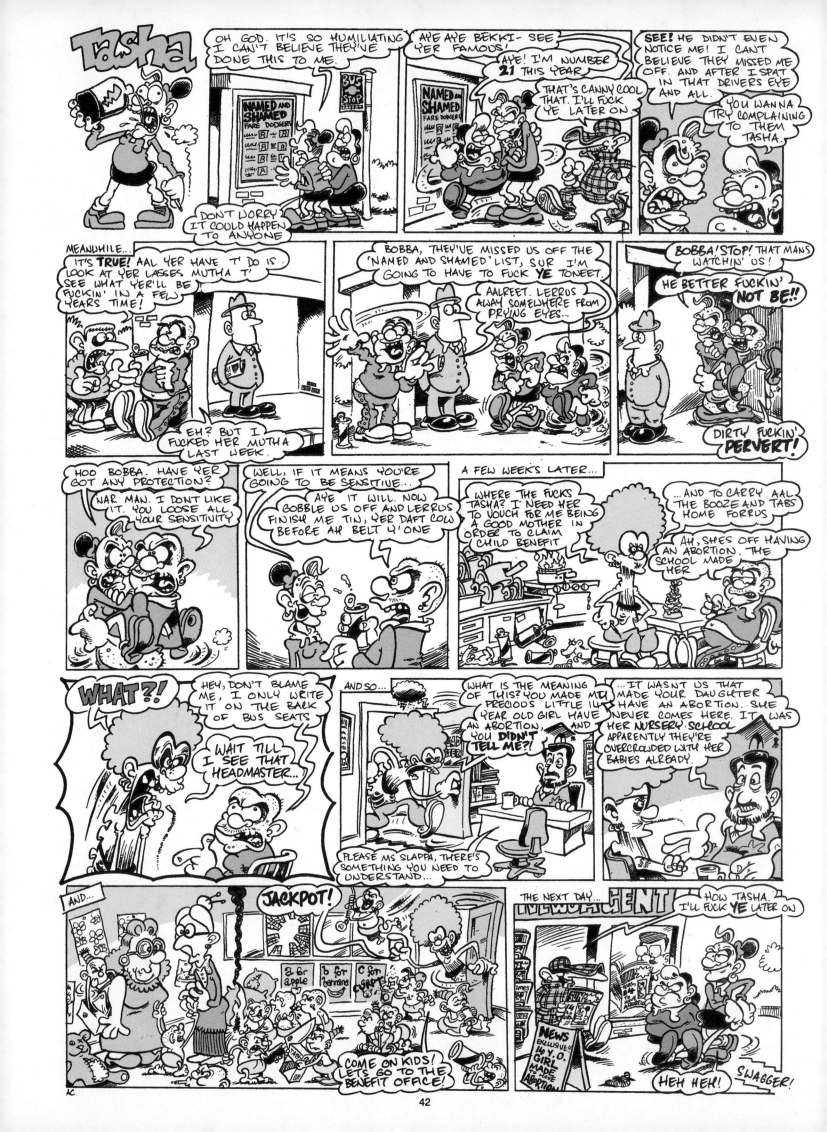

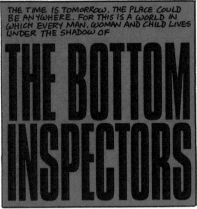
THE TIME IS TOMORROW. THE PLACE COULD BE ANYWHERE. FOR THIS IS A WORLD IN WHICH EVERY MAN, WOMAN AND CHILD LIVES UNDER THE SHADOW OF

THE BOTTOM INSPECTORS

A WORLD IN WHICH A KNOCK AT THE DOOR CAN HERALD THE BEGINNING OF A NIGHTMARE WHICH WILL NEVER END...

KNOCK KNOCK

I WONDER WHO THAT CAN BE.

OH, HELLO. IT'S JIMMY SMITH, ISN'T IT? MY WORD, ARE YOU IN THE CUB SCOUTS NOW?

YES MRS ROBERTS.

WE'RE WORKING TO GET OUR GOOD CONDUCT BADGES. MAY WE HELP YOU WITH YOUR HOUSEWORK?

WHY YES, THAT'S VERY KIND OF YOU. PLEASE COME IN, CHILDREN

THANK YOU MRS ROBERTS.

DARLING, I'M HOME.

LATER

HELLO DEAR. I'M JUST TAKING THESE BOYS SOME MILK AND BISCUITS ~ THEY'VE BEEN WORKING EVER SO HARD.

BOYS? WHAT BOYS... OH MY GOD! WHAT DID YOU LET THEM IN FOR?!

ARE YOU MAD? GET THEM OUT OF HERE NOW!

'BYE FOR NOW, MR ROBERTS

SWEET JESUS...

DARLING, WHAT'S THE MATTER? THAT WAS MARY SMITH'S LITTLE BOY ~ THEY'RE JUST CUB SCOUTS.

NOT JUST CUB SCOUTS ~ EAGLE BROWN EYE SCOUTS! IT'S THE YOUNG PERSON'S ORGANISATION SET UP BY THE BOTTOM INSPECTORS TO SPY ON FAMILIES AND FRIENDS, AND REPORT ANY SUSPICIONS OF BOTTOM CRIME

GASP!

OTHERWISE KNOWN AS THE BOTTLER YOUTH!

EB ES LAVATORY SURVEILLANCE JOB DONE

MY GOD! I WONDERED WHY THEY WERE ONLY INTERESTED IN CLEANING THE BATHROOM

WE HAVEN'T GOT LONG! THERE'S NO TIME TO PACK OUR SUITCASES ~ WE'LL HAVE TO GET OUT OF HERE...

..STRAIGHT AWAY

NOT LEAVING US ARE YOU, MR ROBERTS? NO. OF COURSE NOT.

EAGLE BROWN EYE SCOUT SMITH ~ REPORT YOUR SURVEILLANCE OBSERVATIONS.

YES SIR OBERBOTTOMFUHRER.

IN THE SUBJECT'S BATHROOM WE NOTED THAT THE LOO ROLL HAD AT SOME TIME FALLEN INTO THE TOILET AND THEN BEEN DRIED OUT, RENDERING THE FABRIC OF THE PAPER UNSTABLE.

B- BUT THAT'S NOT AN OFFENCE AGAINST BOTTOM LAW!

MAYBE NOT. BUT IT CAN FACILITATE A MOST SERIOUS BOTTOM CRIME...

..AS WE SHALL SEE WHEN YOU BARE YOUR BOTTOM!

JUST SO! THE UNSTABLE PAPER HAS PARTIALLY DISINTEGRATED DURING WIPING, RESULTING IN FRAGMENTS OF IT ADHERING TO YOUR BOTTOM CLEFT.

DIXCEL DETRITUS IS A SECTION TWO BOTTOM OFFENCE, CARRYING TEN YEARS IN A BOTTOM REHABILITATION UNIT.

WE ALSO NOTED THAT IN THE LAUNDRY BASKET, MRS ROBERTS' UNDERPANTS BORE TRACES OF NETTLE POLLEN

HM. NOW I WONDER WHY THAT SHOULD BE, MRS ROBERTS?

COULD IT BE THAT YOU WERE CAUGHT SHORT WHEN OUT IN THE COUNTRYSIDE, AND OBLIGED TO RELIEVE YOUR BLADDER WHILST SQUATTING IN THE UNDERGROWTH?

Y-YES ~ WE HAD A PICNIC IN THE WOODS ON SUNDAY...

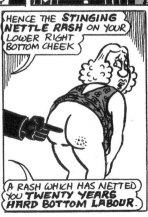
HENCE THE STINGING NETTLE RASH ON YOUR LOWER RIGHT BOTTOM CHEEK

A RASH WHICH HAS NETTED YOU TWENTY YEARS HARD BOTTOM LABOUR.

TAKE THEM AWAY! THEIR IMPERFECT BOTTOMS HAVE NO PLACE IN OUR LEADER'S PLANS FOR A GLORIOUS THOUSAND-YEAR BOTTOM REICH.

NO.. PLEASE!

IF YOUR BOTTOM IS PIMPLED OR FLABBY AND DIMPLED IF YOUR CLEFT-HAIR IS NOT WINNET-FREE

IF INADEQUATE WIPING HAS CAUSED GUSSET-STRIPING YOUR BOTTOM BELONGS, YOUR BOTTOM BELONGS, YOUR BOTTOM BELONGS TO ME

In a spot of bother and need a brief?...come on down to

The BARRISTER WAREHOUSE

SUMMER CLEARANCE SALE NOW ON!

TOP QUALITY LEGAL ADVICE AT ROCK BOTTOM PRICES!!!!!!!!

JUST LOOK AT THESE PRICES!

Mike Mansfield QC.
was £300 per hour
NOW only £249.99 per hour*

His Hnr. Lord Denning QC.
was £350 per hour
NOW only £299.99 per hour*

Clive Anderson QC.
was £150 per hour
NOW only £99.99 per hour*

*or part thereof

SPECIAL OFFER!
Spend £1000 or more before the end of July and you'll receive an ambiguously worded and totally unfathomable 20-page document **ABSOLUTELY FREE!**

WE ARE HERE

What's the charge....?

It's lower than you might think at *Allied QCs!*

- Petty hedge dispute with neighbour — £8000
- Misunderstanding over father's will — £2500
- Worthless local authority search — £1000
- 3 phone calls to other solicitor — £850
- Acrimonious divorce — £8500

SPECIAL OFFER!
Hire one of our QCs to defend you on a burglary charge and we'll represent a friend on a charge of ABH absolutely **FREE!**

Offer ends 25th July

Allied QCs
Lord Denning Industrial Estate, Ring Road, Fulchester

The LOWEST legal costs in town?
We plead GUILTY!

DALLAS SOLICITORS

1000s of barristers all under one roof!

Specific representation from just £9.99 per minute, plus hundreds of advice remnants*

*All prices are exclusive of VAT and disbursments

OPEN 7 DAYS A WEEK!

Just off the Ringroad next to Silks 'R' Us

Mickle & Muckle

Keep track of your huge fees

When Time is Money, every second counts.

Mickle & Muckle Ltd, legal Chronometers are proud to present their new

Solicitor's Timepiece

£199

Takes just **20 seconds** a day to wind. That's just £3.30 of your time! (+ VAT)

Accurate to 30 pence per year!

Mickle & Muckle Lawyers' Timepieces since 1896

"Before I had my Mickle and Muckle Solicitor's watch, I had a cheap Japanese one. The battery went flat during a consultation with a client, the meeting overran by four minutes and I was four grand out of pocket." *M.M, QC.*

Tired of lugging that heavy wallet?
...get yourself a solicitor's

Walletbarrow
NEW

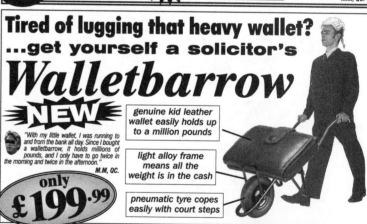

"With my little wallet, I was running to and from the bank all day. Since I bought a walletbarrow, it holds millions of pounds, and I only have to go twice in the morning and twice in the afternoon." *M.M, QC.*

only £199.99

- genuine kid leather wallet easily holds up to a million pounds
- light alloy frame means all the weight is in the cash
- pneumatic tyre copes easily with court steps

Since 1995, barristers have sworn by the mysterious aquitting power of

the Lucky Glove of O.J.

Only £10 each

Talisman shown larger and luckier than actual size of 3mm

This charm, blessed by Gypsy Hayden-Williams, seventh solicitor of a seventh solicitor will ensure you win every case that goes to court.

A talisman which bestows GREAT FORTUNE upon defence counsels

"My client was accused of murdering Jill Dando which he never and was stitched up like a kipper. If I'd only of known about the Lucky Glove of OJ, he'd be free to rollerskate the streets of Fulham today"
M.M, QC.

"I represented the Birmingham Six who spent 21 years inside. The day before the Law Lords' hearing I bought the Lucky Glove of OJ. The next day their convictions were quashed flat as pancakes!"
B.B, QC.

Please send me ___ OJ's glove talismans.
Name_____ QC. Address_____
Send £10 for each + £2.99 for p&p and disbursments to Glove, PO Box 8, Leeds.

---

the NOOSE of PIERREPOINT
prosecutor's talisman

just £7.99 each

In shops NOW!

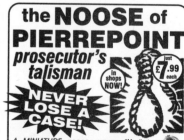

NEVER LOSE A CASE!

A MINIATURE noose, woven from fibres of the **ACTUAL ROPE** used to hang sweet factory burglar Derek Bentley, the Noose of Pierrepoint will bestow luck upon prosecuting counsels and ensure a conviction even on the flimsiest of evidence.

"My client was found guilty of murdering Jill Dando which he never and was stitched up like a kipper. The prosecutor later told me that he had a Noose of Pierrepoint in his pocket throughout the trial!"
M.M, QC.

SCURVY DOGG

WELL SNOOP DOGG, I'VE GOOD NEWS AND BAD NEWS...

THE GOOD NEWS IS YOUR CAREER AS AN AMERICAN RAP GIANT CONTINUES TO SOAR, WITH A ROLE IN THE RECENT 'SOUL PLANE' FILM AND A HIGHLY-ANTICIPATED NEW CD REUNITING YOU WITH LEGENDARY HIP-HOP SUPERGROUP '213'...

THE BAD NEWS IS YOUR GUMS ARE ROTTING AWAY FROM CHRONIC LACK OF VITAMIN C.

I'M AFRAID ALL YOUR TEETH ARE GOING TO FALL OUT UNLESS YOU GET SOME VITAMIN C BY — OH, LET'S SAY ONE O'CLOCK.

FO' SHIZZLE, MY NIZZLE — THAT'S AN *HOUR* FROM NOW!!

CHRIZZLE ON A BIZZLE! I'D BEST GIVE A SHOUT OUT TO THE PEEPS IN MY POSSE TO BRING ME SOME VITAMIN C-RICH FRUITS AND VEGGIES PRONTIZZLE!

YO YO SNOOP — I GOT YOUR CHOPPERS SORTED PROPER! HERE'S A *WHOLE CASE OF FRUIT!*

FAB-O-RIZZLE! IT'S MY GANGSTA PAL 50 CENT!

FRUIT

WHAT THE —?!?

BANANAS?!? DAAAAMN, FOOL! THEM 'NANAS IS A GOOD DIETARY SOURCE OF *POTASSIUM* AND B6, NOT NO DAMN VITAMIN C!

NOW TAKE THESE AWAY BEFORE I BUST A CAP IN YOUR *DAMN FOOL ASS!*

I MEAN HONESTLY, WHAT KIND OF DAFT CUNIZZLE — ...BUGGER, THERE GOES MY SECOND BICUSPID.

YO SNOOP!

POP!

WHY, IT'S ONE OF MY *SKANKY HO'S!*

WHEN I GOT YA HOLLA, I WAS BUMPIN' DA NASTY ON MY BOOTY (OR SOME SUCH THING) WITH THE LOCAL COSTERMONGER — SO I STOLE HIS BARROW! ALL THESE *LOVELY GREEN LEAFIES* SHOULD FIX YOUR CHICLETS!

FRESH PRODUCE

WAAA! *ICEBERG LETTUCE?!* YO BITCH — DON'T YOU KNOW ICEBERG HAS *MINIMAL NUTRITIONAL VALUE?* IT'S THE *DARK LEAFY GREENS* LIKE *SPINACH, KALE,* AND *BRUSSELS SPROUTS* THAT ARE HIGH IN VITAMIN C, AS WELL AS FOLIC ACID AND BONE-BUILDING NUTRIENTS LIKE CALCIUM AND VITAMIN K!

I OUGHTA *SLAP* YO — CRAP — THAT ONE'S AN INCISOR.

BUT SNOOP — HOW ARE WE SUPPOSED TO KNOW ALL THIS VITAMIN SHEEE-IT?

POINK!

DAAAMN, DO I HAVE TO TEACH Y'ALL THE FOOD STANDARD AGENCY'S 'BALANCE OF GOOD HEALTH' GUIDE AGAIN?? NOW LOOK —

YO, SNOOP!!

FLAMBOYANT CHICAGO PIMP *ARCHBISHOP DON 'MAGIC' JUAN!*

YO DEE! SOON AS I GOT THE 4-1-1 I LOADED THE BOOT OF MY ENORMOUS PIMP-STYLE PINK CADILLAC FULL OF *POTATOES* AND CAME STRAIGHT TO YOUR CRIB!

B ATCH

FIZZLE ME *RIZZLED!* ONE SPUD CONTAINS 45% OF THE DAILY REQUIREMENT OF VITAMIN C! MY PEARLIES IS *SAVED!!*

WORD UP! AND I'D HAVE BEEN HERE SOONER ONLY IT TOOK AGES TO PEEL 'EM ALL! GAAH! NO! NO! NO!!! THE VITAMINS ARE IN THE SKINS!!

LISTEN, YOU *STUPID GODDIZZLE MUTHA-FIZZLING TWIZZLERS!!!* I NEED *CITRUS FRUIT* — LIKE *LIMES, ORANGES AND TANGERINES!!!*

DOIK!

WELL...

PING!

...I DO HAVE THIS LEMON THAT I SUCK ON TO KEEP MY MOUTH LOOKING LIKE A CAT'S ARSE...

YESYESYES! THAT'S IT!! GIMME!!

GIMME!!

HA-HAAA! I'M JUST IN TIME — IT'S NOT GONE ONE YET! ALL I HAVE TO DO IS EAT THIS LEMON AND —

BONGGG!!

PING! TING! POING! KA-TOING! etc.

...BUGGIZZLE.

NEXT DAY, IN EVERY SUBURBAN SHOPPING CENTRE ON EARTH...

POINTSTRETCHAZZT!

GNASHA OR SMASHAZ

YO YO MA PEEPFF — WHAPFF DA WORBB?

FFUP, PWAYA! JUFF GUMMIN' WIF MA HOMIEFF!

AIGHT!

R·H '04

47

The Ang

"I fear a new murder spree has only just begun" says psychic Doris

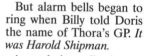

KILLER DOC *Harold Shipman* has finally done the decent thing by hanging himself in his cell, bringing his 20-year reign of terror to an end... *or so everyone thought.* Because now a leading psychic says that the bearded medic's death may only be the start of a new murder spree... this time *in the afterlife.*

Spiritual medium Doris Mandeville fears that dead Shipman has wasted no time in setting himself up as a GP in Heaven. And now, with hundreds of late old women on his books, he's already getting up to his old tricks.

She told us: "If nothing is done to stop him, the bodies will soon be piling up in heaven just like they did in Hyde."

Mandeville's suspicions were first aroused during a

EXCLUSIVE!

routine seance at her Doncaster home.

gossip

"I was having a chat with my red indian guide Billy Two Rivers. He was filling me in on all the gossip from the other side when he mentioned that the late Thora Hird had died unexpectedly.

"I was surprised, because I'd been chatting to Thora

on my ouija board a couple of days earlier and she seemed full of beans. Billy

told me that she'd fallen off her stairlift and had been found dead by her doctor.

Nelson's

Doris was immediately suspicious. She told us: "I knew there was no way in this world or the next that Thora would fall off her stairlift. She was an expert who had appeared in over 5,000 Churchill adverts and she knew what she was doing."

But alarm bells began to ring when Billy told Doris the name of Thora's GP. *It was Harold Shipman.*

A week later Doris was making lunch when she made contact with Two Rivers again.

"I was having trouble getting a souffle to rise, so I asked Billy to get in touch with my old friend Fanny Craddock for some advice.

However, he got to her house in Heaven just in time to see her coffin being carried out of the front door.

Fanny

"Her husband, the late Johnny Craddock, explained that Fanny had re-died unexpectedly whilst visiting the doctor for her yearly flu jab. My blood ran cold when Billy told me the doc-

---

You Only Die Twice

A CLOUD OF SUSPICION hangs over a series of mysterious sudden deaths which have taken place at Dr Shipman's Heaven surgery, says Doris. Here's just a few of the perfectly healthy dead people who have suddenly shuffled off their immortal coils whilst visiting the evil late GP's spirit.

Queen Boadicea
The legendary warrior Queen of the Iceni people killed herself in AD61 after suffering defeat at the hands of Roman invaders. Two weeks ago, she visited Shipman in Heaven complaining of piles. The doctor made a routine housecall the next morning, and Boadicea was found dead - apparently from a massive heart attack - when her husband Jules Verne returned home from work that evening.
Verdict: *Natural Causes*

Florence Nightingale
The bedridden Crimean War veteran who died in 1910 was a popular figure about Heaven, where she was known as 'The angel with the lamp". She was found dead once more just two hours after a home visit from the doctor. Shipman had been called in by neighbours

Rod Hull and Emu, who had seen her earlier that morning. Nightingale told them she was concerned she might be getting shingles. "Other than that she seemed fine," Hull told an inquest, just before Emu grabbed the coroner's testicles and wrestled him to the ground.
Verdict: *Open*

Mrs Mills
The seventies pub piano favourite died in 1982 of following a series of strokes. In early February of this year she felt twinges of arthritis in one of her wings and made an appointment to see the late Dr Shipman. He gave her a pain-killing injection and she returned home. Later, complaining of dizziness, she took to her bed where she was found dead next morning.
Verdict: *Natural Causes*

Pat Coombs
The Celebrity Squares dullard had only been up in Heaven for a few months when she visited Shipman's surgery for a routine smear test. According to Shipman, she started becoming short of breath. She became hysterical and started to panic like she did in On The Buses when Stan put spiders on the bus, quickly turned blue and died.
Verdict: *Open*

Dandy Nicholls
The Till Death Us Do Part "silly old moo" called in at the doctor's surgery to have her passport photograph signed. According to Shipman, he went to his cupboard to get a pen and when he turned round she was dead, apparently of a massive heart attack.
Verdict: *Natural Causes*

Doris (left) and (main picture) at one of her seances, yesterday

tor's name. It was the late Harold Shipman again.

The unexpected deaths of Thora Hird and Fanny Craddock were bad enough. But nothing prepared Doris for Billy Two Rivers' next bombshell. HRH the late Queen Mother had also just "dropped dead" again, whilst having her bunions shaved at the doctor's surgery. *Mandeville didn't need to be told the doctor's name.*

"To lose the country's favourite granny once was bad enough, but to lose her again - and this time to a dead mass-murderer like Shipman - was the last straw. I decided to go to the police with my suspicions."

pancake

But whilst Doncaster Police were concerned when they heard the medium's horrifying story, they were powerless to act. Doris told us: "They said that they could only investigate crimes that took place on this side of the astral veil. They assured me that all officers had been briefed on my allegations and that the first one to die would launch a thorough investigation as soon as he got to the Pearly Gates."

Liz Hurley

But Doris was far from satisfied with the response.

"That's not good enough," she stormed. "We could be waiting for ages, and all the while Shipman's on another killing spree in the afterlife. Surely the police have got at least one detective who's terminally ill or at least depressed who wouldn't mind doing himself in and going up there to catch him red-handed."

"And this time they should hang him. And I'll kill myself and pull the ruddy lever," she added.

Littlejohn

"Afterlife should MEAN afterlife"

Page 52

Angels with Dirty Secrets

WITH NO PRISONS in Heaven, even the worst criminals are free to roam the streets of Paradise, rubbing shoulders with angels who've never broken a law in their lives. So what has happened to Britain's late killers? We ask...

Where Are They Now?

Cromwell Street murderer **Fred West** has a thriving building business. He recently put an extension on a cloud for *Eric Morecambe*, and erected a carport for *St Thomas Aquinas*.

Cockney killers the **Kray twins** run a successful chain of perfume shops, called *Heaven Scent*. However, dead police believe that this business is merely a front, laundering cash for a series of drugs cartels.

Gay US cannibal **Jeffrey Dahmer** found it hard to fit in when he got to heaven. After working as a pub cellarman, night watchman and singing telegram he became a busker. He can now be found most weekdays, playing his banjo for coppers outside the Pearly Gates.

19th century prostitute slasher **Jack the Ripper** now works as a salesman in one of Heaven's largest carpet warehouses. These days he is reluctant to talk about his killing spree in the backstreets of Victorian London. *"Those murders were a long time ago,"* he told us. *"And I'm not going to say who I am, either. That was a secet I took with me to my grave."*

Bloodthirsty **Vlad the Impaler**, personally responsible for over 30,000 deaths in 13th century Transylvania, is now a reformed character. He spends each day selling brushes and household cleaning goods door to door, and in the evenings teaches information technology at a local Further Education College.

Genocidal Nazi **Adolf Hitler** has certainly calmed down since his Nuremberg Rally heyday. A neighbour told us: *"We don't see much of him to be honest. He keeps himself to himself, but he always smiles and says hello if you walk past when he's mowing his cloud."*

Sex-bomb killer **Ruth Ellis**, unlike other dead murderers, is safely behind bars in Heaven. But she's not in prison - she pulls pints at *Cloud 9*, a swanky wine bar owned by 17th century diarist *Samuel Pepys!*

49

Letterbocks

Letterbocks, Viz Comic, PO Box 1PT, Newcastle upon Tyne NE99 1PT

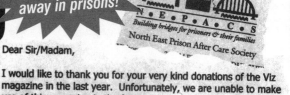

According to Nietzsche, 'That which does not kill me makes me stronger'. I'm sure my grandad would not agree. He suffered a series of massive strokes in the early '90s which have left him an incontinent vegetable for the past 12 years.

**A Thorne
Sandbach**

They say "you can't judge a book by its cover". What nonsense. The last edition of *High School Anal* that I bought featured a young lady stuffing a big one up her bomb-bay on the front page, and this turned out to be an excellent indication of the contents.

Mark Roberts, e-mail

Predictably, the moaning minnies have been quick to voice their disapproval of the government's decision not to deprive Jeffrey Archer of his seat in the Lords. However, it

In this space age you can electromail your letters and tips to letters@viz.co.uk

seems to me that they are missing the point. The value of the Second Chamber is surely that the peers are able to bring their particular areas of experience to bear on legislative matters. Lord Archer's unparalleled expertise in the areas of going with whores and lying on oath will undoubtedly prove to be worth their weight in gold should those subjects come up in a Parliamentary debate.

**T. Culkin
Douglas, Isle of Man**

I am appalled that the government proposes to hold a referendum on the new European constitution. We already pay the MPs' inflated wages, and now they want us to do their jobs for them. I work in a crisp factory, and if we simply handed our customers a potato and told them to do it themselves, we'd soon find ourselves out of work.

As usual, it's one law for the politicians and another for the people who make crisps.

**H. Gorman
Yeovil**

My dad told me on his deathbed that if he could have his life all over again, he wouldn't change a single thing. I sharply reminded him of the holiday in Mablethorpe in the early seventies where he slipped in a huge dog turd and ended up throwing a perfectly good pair of suede shoes in a litter bin on the seafront. As I pointed out to him, surely to God he wouldn't want to go through that again. Needless to say, he had no answer to that, and died a few minutes later.

**H Bentink
Nottingham**

I saw this ad in my local paper. Needless to say I didn't go, even though I've got lots under my hammer. Whatever that means.

**D. Chadwick
Bodmin**

NGA - MARCH 2004   Comments, Adver

LET'S GO OUT - MOTHERING

SMEGMA CHARITY AUCTION NIGHT
at *The Merrymoor*, Mawgan Porth
at 8pm on Saturday 13th March
e prizes. Any gifts or unwanted Christmas presents fo

I'm 86 and the other day a youth on the bus refused to give up his seat for me, and I had to stand for the whole journey. What a fool I

felt when I realised that it was my own fault as, 60 years ago, I joined up and fought Hitler for that young man's right to sit wherever he wanted on the bus. If I'd have known then how my selfless bravery in the North Africa campaign would come to backfire on me, I would have fought for the Nazis.

**Albert Sparks
Englefield**

In this year's Rich List, Michael Owen was named as the second wealthiest British footballer. I can't help feeling that if he wasted less time on playing football and devoted more time earning money he might improve his position.

**Mrs Oscar Peterson,
Prague**

It's all very well these bleeding heart liberals getting on their high horses because the Canadians are culling seals again. They don't have a troupe of seals living next door to them, like

I do. If, like me, they were kept awake every night by incessant clapping and the honking of bicycle horns into the early hours, they'd be the first onto the ice floe with a baseball bat, let me tell you.

**A. Forrest
Castleford**

Every time I see David Beckham shaking hands with a referee or captain of an opposing teams, I can't help thinking that he's using the same hand with which he manually stimulated the bisexual genitals of Rebecca Loos. Unless, of course, he did it with his left hand. Either way, I think we should be told, to set the nation's mind at rest once and for all.

**L. Pattinson
Leeds**

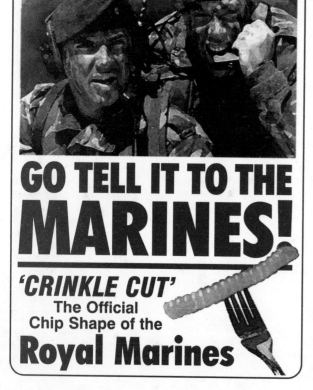

HEY, THE PEOPLE ON THE GROUND LOOK LIKE ANTS

Look at this little bus I saw recently. If any reader has seen a smaller bus, I'll eat my hat.

G. Gladstone, Newcastle

I couldn't sleep the other night so my wife suggested that I try counting sheep jumping over a 5-bar gate. I drove around all night looking for a flock able to perform this feat, but I hadn't found one by the time the sun came up. Needless to say I got even less sleep that night than usual.

A. Morris, Frampton

Thanks to the politically correct lobby, it is now considered perfectly acceptable for "gays" to join the Fire Brigade. Well, the next time the alarm goes off at the station, I only hope there isn't one of these perverts standing at the bottom of the pole with his gentleman out, waiting for one of his colleagues to slide onto it, that's all I can say.

Major U. Hepscott-White (retd), Aldershot

In spite of all the threats to our democracy, it's good to know that we still live in a society where a woman can suck off the Captain of the national football team, and then be given an hour of prime-time telly give her side of the story.

Mrs Turpin, Hull

TOP TIPS

TRAMPS. Watch *Ray Mears' World of Survival* in Dixon's window to open your eyes to a whole host of natural foodstuffs.
Daniel Green, e-mail

DOG LOVERS. Reduce your chances of going blind by only buying brown or black labradors.
Ian E., Glasgow

HOTELIERS. Save money on expensive promotions. Simply christen your daughter with the name of your hotel, film her having sex, and release the footage on the internet. Hey presto - instant worldwide advertising!
P. Ming, Paris

HOUSEWIVES. Add washing up liquid to your recipies so as you can cook and wash up at the same time.
Sam, e-mail

MUMS. Make bath nights more fun for the kids by playing 'moth aircraft carrier'. Simply float a shoebox in the bath with a torch attached. Leave a window open for ten minutes, then turn off the bathroom lights and watch as the moths attempt to make their dramatic and dangerous landings.
A Hall, e-mail

BACHELORS. Have silicone breast implants put in your penis so you can give yourself a tit-fuck.
J. Rigby, Chorley

ORIGAMI ENTHUSIASTS. Save money on expensive brown paper by simply folding Happy Shopper beefburgers. Also your final model can also be grilled, filling your house with the pleasing aroma of tramps' socks.
A. Morris, London

RAY MEARS. Lose those extra pounds by not constantly grazing on grass and leaves like some kind of prize-winning cow.
Daniel Green, e-mail

DON'T waste money on a new car with air-conditioning. Simply buy one that has been in a 'death crash' and let the ghosts keep you cool.
Russ, Sheringham

Socks of the Best

We asked over a thousand celebrities and six ordinary people what sort of socks they liked best... Here's what the STARS said.

Former Blue Peter prop forward **Katy Hill**.
"Argyll socks. Yes."

Wife-of-Bryan McFadden **Kerry McFadden**.
"'Tis Argyll socks I'll be wanting."

Moustachioed understudy's friend **Martine McCutcheon**
"Argyll socks are luverly."

Pool death gay funnyman **Michael Barrymore**
"I don't like all-white socks, but Argyll socks are aw-wight by me."

Checkout-hogging right hand side of the TV Quick logo **Jessie Wallace** (Kat Slater)
"Argyll socks, thanks."

Plum-faced, doll-voiced wobbly style-dodger **Kirsty Allsopp** from Location Location Location
"Argyll socks."

Posh pop gibbon **Charlie Eyebrows** from Busted
"Yeah. Socks. Argyll ones."

Fat Cunt **Bernard Manning**
"Argyll socks."

Cunt **Jim Davidson**
"Argyll socks."

Odds Bodkins

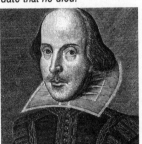

How to beat the bookie with the Viz Tipster, Oddsworth Bodkins

● **HERE's** a hot tip - phone your bookie and ask him what odds he'll give you that *Bob Monkhouse*, *Marilyn Monroe* and *Jason Donovan* all share the same birthday. He should give you at least 133,000 to 1, because that's the chances of such an unlikely thing happening. But get this...they were all born on June 1st! Put £8 down on the triple accumulator, and you'll walk out with a cool million in your back bin. *But remember to pay the tax first!*

● **LADBROKES** are currently offering 35-1 that Shakespeare died on his birthday. Not brilliant odds but well worth a flutter, because a little bird tells me that Shakespeare was born on April 23rd - the exact same date that he died!

Tip of the Week

● **THEY SAY** a fool and his money are soon parted. Well here's a way to make a fool out of your bookmaker and net yourself a tidy wedge into the bargain. Go up to the counter and say:
"Antidisestablishmentarianism is a very long word, but I bet I can spell it."
Any bookie worth his salt will give you at least 7-2. Stick a tenner on, and then say:
"I - T" That's thirty-five quid plus your stake! It's like taking candy from a baby.

STUMP UP A FIVER

● **THE BRITISH** Medical Association are conducting a survey to find the average number of legs people have got. And just look at these odds on the Betfair.com website ~
"Average number of legs per person in Great Britain. More than 2; 17-5. Exactly 2; Evens fav. Less than 2; 50-1 bar."
I've had an insider's tip from a mate who works in a hospital. He says there's plenty of amputees to bring the average down under 2, but there's not very many 3-legged freaks to push it back up! I haven't done the maths, but I reckon that 50-1 shot's got to be worth a flutter. I've stuck a fiver on it and I suggest you do the same. *But hurry, the result's in next Tuesday.*

● **GO INTO** William Hill and ask what the odds are on a year NOT lasting 365 days. Last time I tried this scam I got 50-1. After placing your bet reveal you were talking about a year on Mars, which lasts 687 days! £1000 profit for a £20 stake? Nice work if you can get it!

● *TALKING* about years, place a bet that your grandad is over 500 years old. You can expect odds of between 600 and 1000-1. When you've placed your bet, introduce your 72-year-old grandad and explain that you were talking about DOG YEARS, making him 504! Two grand for the price of a pint? I'll have a bit of that!

● **FINALLY**, Victor Chandler online are currently offering a tasty 15-4 that the widow of water speed ace *Donald Campbell* isn't married to *Greengrass* out of Heartbeat. Sounds like a risky punt, doesn't it. But get this, an insider has tipped off Odds Bodkins that Mrs Campbell and Greengrass actor *Bill Maynard* are in fact *man and wife!* At those odds it's a 24-carat steal - you'll trouser a cool £30 for an £8 stake. Get your bets in quick!

More top tips next time, gamble fans!

Littlejohn

e-mail: notgayjustcurious@the-sun.co.uk

MULTI-murderer Harold Shipman tops himself in Wakefield Prison. The next day he's large as life in spirit world, practising as a GP.

He must think he's died and gone to Heaven. Which he has.

And by Heaven I don't mean "Sir" Richard Branson's gay nightclub, where grown men in leather shorts are encouraged to rub baby oil into each other's lithe buttocks before indulging in unnatural sex acts.

These sodomites claim they're just as God made them.

Well God made Adam and Eve, not Adam and Steve...and Julian and Sandy and Quentin and Larry

Afterlife should MEAN Afterlife!

and Barrymore, all writhing about in some huge sodomitic daisy chain, thrusting their engorged manhoods backwards and forwards, backwards and forwards like the pistons of a huge gay steam train. In and out they go. In and out, in and out, harder and harder and faster and faster until they finally explode in a twisted, spent heap of sweating homosexual ecstasy.

No. I'm talking about Heaven. The land in the clouds where Granny goes when she shuffles off her mortal coil. Life everlasting? Not in Tony Blair's Britain.

Not with dead murderers like Harold Shipman free to ply their evil trade on the streets of Paradise.

Doctor Death's spirit should have been arrested the moment it floated

free of his earthly remains and taken straight to HM Prison Heaven. The ghosts of murderers like Shipman should be locked up for the rest of their supernatural lives.

But will it happen? Well, of course it will.

The day George Bush and Saddam Hussein announce they're getting married.

Which, if they were gay, wouldn't surprise me at all. God made Saddam and Eve, not Saddam and Steve. You couldn't make it up. It's political correctness gone mad.

Heaven's going to Hell in a handcart.

Jay Okay after Bear Scare

Bear scare survivor, Jay, yestereday (left). And Big bear (main picture, right) and little bear (main picture left). Middle size bear not shown.

IT was nearly Emergency on Planet Earth for big-hatted pop king Jamiroquai when his rental car broke down on holiday in Peru.

Speaking exclusively to the *Lima Telegraph and Argus* about his lucky escape, the plucky Space Cowboy told how he went looking for help in the woods and found a funny little house.

bufallo

"There was, like, no-one home, so I thought I'd go in and have a sniff around," he said. "And on the back of the door were three buffalo hats – a great big hat, a middling-sized hat and a teeny tiny hat.

Jay, real name Jamiroquai Kay tried on the hats, but found one was too furry and one wasn't furry enough. Luckily, the last one was just right. He said: "I was, like, made up."

The Stretford-born funkwit then stumbled into a dark room. And he was in for a shock when he found the light switch!

springfield

"It was a triple garage, with three red Ferraris in it – a great big Ferrari, a middling-sized Ferrari and a teeny tiny Ferrari.

"I had a quick burn around the woods in all of them," he told the paper. "One was too fast, one was too slow, but the third one was just right. I was, like, sorted!"

But the millionaire hat-and-Ferrari enthusiast, famous for his big collections of hats and Ferraris was in for an even bigger shock when he found the bedroom.

massachusetts

"There were three beds, each with a blonde in it – a great big blonde, a middling-sized blonde and a teeny tiny blonde.

"So I made love with each of them – one was too hard, one was too soft, but one was just right. I was, like, this is the best holiday I've ever had!"

But disaster struck as he was enjoying a nookie-style romp with the teeny tiny blonde.

"I froze to the spot," recalls J, real name Jay. "I looked up to see this great big bear, this middling-sized bear and this teeny tiny bear standing by the door staring at me.

"And the great big bear boomed in his great big voice, 'Who's been sleeping in my blonde?' and I thought, uh-oh, time to get out of here, Jamiroquai."

In a hat-raising dash to safety, the distinctive pop star, son of Cilla Black impressionist Karen Kay, did his trademark loony leap over the beds and through a closed window, plunging a terrifying metre and a half to safety.

"I belted the hell out of there like a man running over hot rocks," he admitted. "But as I was scarpering, I could hear the teeny tiny bear saying, 'It's all right – it's just Jamiroquai,' so maybe I should've stuck around!"

Following his ordeal, Jamiroquai, real name James Iroquai, cancelled his band's tour of South America and the Falkland Islands. He is now recovering in his £6 million, 10 bedroom hat in Surrey.

The Tim Henman Story — Part 1

Wimbledon Royal Infirmary, 6th Sept 1974...

I can see the baby's head, Mrs Henman. He's nearly out your fanny

Come on, Tim! Come on, Tim!

At school, Tim wasn't interested in his lessons and spent many hours daydreaming...

What's seven eights? Come on, Tim! Come on, Tim! It's very simple

God! Maths is boring

When I leave school, I want to join the Pro-tennis circuit, get thrown out of my first Wimbledon championship and fail to get past the quarter finals every year thereafter

And twenty years later on the Centre Court, that dream came true every year.

Fault!

Game, set and match to Vlodivoskovitch

Yes! I've crashed out in the quarter finals again

Come on, Tim! Let's go home

OH, LORDY! IT'S THE FAT SLAGS

JAPANESE SPECIAL INTEREST

THE MODERN PARENTS

John Fardell

Thanks!

Just a minute. Before we decide if we're going to give you a lift, you'll need to answer a few **questions**... One can't be too careful...

Have you ever been convicted of a **violent crime?** Not including Anti-Globalisation direct action, obviously. Nor justified suicide bombing by oppressed peoples.

No, no. I've never been arrested for anything.

15 minutes later...

Have you ever been fox hunting? Have you ever worn fur?

Have you ever had **misogynist fantasies** whilst masturbating?

I.. er.. um...

30 minutes later...

Hmm... You **seem** to be safe enough... But obviously, as a White Male, you can't sit in the back with the children...

...and obviously you can't sit in the front if Malcolm's driving, because it would be **sexist** to have both men in the front and the woman in the back.

She's right... **I'd better** go in the back and Cressida can drive.

Absolutely...

Just because I haven't jumped through the hoops of some patriarchal Establishment **driving test** and got one of their **Fascist driving licences**, doesn't mean I can't drive.

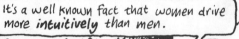

It's a well known fact that women drive more **intuitively** than men.

VROOOM

SCREECH

BEEEEP!

Of course, Malcolm and I don't actually **agree** with driving motor cars at all.

But I suffer from Sensitive Persons' Disorder Syndrome, so I'm prevented from travelling on our overcrowded, under-funded public transport system.

Obviously, it's all a **conspiracy** by the multinational oil companies to force even environmentally-aware people like us to do their evil polluting for them...

An hour later...

...and we **have** to use the car to take the boys to school because it wouldn't be **safe** for them to walk... So much **traffic** round where we live. All these **selfish** people driving their kids to school when they don't need to.

Time for a snack... Would you like a piece of my homemade flapjack?

BEEEP!

Er...Yeah, that's very kind of you.

Don't worry - there's no sugar or syrup in it. Just wholemeal tree bark, organic lentils and garlic.

I wouldn't eat it. It tastes like poo.

Tarquin!

Tarquin's going through a misplaced- challenge-to- parenting phase at the moment...

Of course, he's **really** trying to challenge Western Society, not us, but he can't see that. His main problem is that his school won't recognise his special educational needs...

Another hour later...

...and so we **demanded** that Tarquin be given an appointment with an educational psychologist and do you know what his teacher said?

I can't think.

She said he was **perfectly normal!**... Said we were trying to invent complexes he didn't have!

No! Really?

I'm **bored**.

Alright, Tarquin. Shall we play a game?

OK... Er...I-Spy?

We don't play I-Spy. It discriminates against the visually impaired community.

Of course.

We play I-Feel.

I'll go first... I **feel**, with my sense of **awareness**, something beginning with **G**.

Er... um... I can't guess.

I feel **Guilt**, for all the **harm** that Man has inflicted on Nature... I mean White Man, obviously.

Obviously.

Right, so that's one point to **me**... Not that we believe in playing competitive games... Now you have a go.

What are you feeling right now?

I couldn't begin to tell you.

Here, maybe you need another piece of flapjack to help you get in touch with your inner self.

Er.. Look, actually I've just remembered I'm not going all the way to London after all...

If you just drop me off here at this next junction, that'll be **great**.

Are you sure? But it's just starting to pour with rain.

I'll be fine... Honest... Thanks for the lift.

Bye, then... Bet you're glad you didn't get picked up by some boring businessman.

©John Fardell '04

57

WHAT SAY WE HAVE A LOOK AT MY FINDINGS?

I THINK YOU'LL FIND THEY MAKE INTERESTING VIEWING

MONDAY, 9.05... THE SUBJECT IS SEEN UP A LADDER EFFECTING REPAIRS TO HIS GUTTERING...

NOTE HOW HE HAS CARRIED THE LADDERS FROM THE SHED EVINCING NO VISIBLE SIGNS OF DISCOMFORT WHATSOEVER

TUESDAY 11.38... SUBJECT ATTENDS LOCAL BOWLING ALLEY... NOTE THE EASE WITH WHICH HE LIFTS A 14Lb BOWLING BALL...

WEDNESDAY 11.42... SUBJECT FILMED IN B&Q CAR PARK LIFTING FOUR BAGS OF SAND AND CEMENT INTO HIS CAR...

13.21, SEEN THROWING A WASH-ING MACHINE INTO A SKIP

THURSDAY 16.54, SUBJECT LIFTS BACK END OF A LORRY FULL OF ANVILS TO RETRIEVE A £5 NOTE UNDER ITS WHEEL

INVASION O' PRIVICY, THAT

YOU'RE FIRED, PLOD...PICK UP YOUR CARDS ON THE WAY OUT

SO... WOTCHA, PLOD. FANCY A GAME?.. A TENNER IN, TWO QUID MINIMUM BID?

SORRY, LADS... THEY'VE GIVE ME THE TIN TACK...

THE TIN TACK? WHAT FOR?..YOU'VE DONE NOWT

AYE! Y'VE BEEN OFF F'SIX MONTH

COME ON, LADS... TILL PLOD GETS HIS JOB BACK, WE'RE ON A GO SLOW!

AYE!

HAVE WE STARTED YET?

AYE

TWO WEEKS LATER...

OH, FUCK IT! ALRIGHT, ALRIGHT, YOU WIN... I'LL TELL HIM HE CAN HAVE HIS JOB BACK, THE LAZY FUCKER

SMASHIN'... RIGHT, LADS... BACK TO FULL SPEED!

AYE!

HAVE WE STARTED, YET?

AYE!

BLOODY BLACKMAILIN' BASTARDS.

DIDDLE-DEE-DEE, DIDDLE-DEE-DEE, DIDDLE-DEE-DEE, DEEEEEEEE!

PLOD SPEAKING...WHAT'S THAT?.. I CAN HAVE ME JOB BACK?.. THAT'S GREAT...

CHEERS, BOSS.

...WHAT?. TOMORROW?

NO... I CAN'T MAKE IT TOMORROW, NO WAY.

IT'S THE STRAIN OF THIS LAST 2 WEEKS...IT'S LEFT ME WI' POST TRAUMATIC STRESS DISORDER...

THE DOC'S PUT ME ON THE SICK FOR AT LEAST

...HOLD ON...

... 8 WEEK BE ALRIGHT, FRANK?

FINE BY ME, PLOD

CHEERS... ONLY DON'T FORGET T' SIGN THE FUCKER THIS TIME, EH?..HEH HEH!

Award Win is 2 GOOD 2 B TRUE!

A schoolgirl from Bracknell in Berkshire was the toast of the British media last night as she celebrated victory at the new BAFTA Text Messaging awards.

12-year old Danielle Lollard, twelve, wowed the judges with her winning message, seen by millions scrolling along the bottom of the screen on ITV2's coverage of *I'm A Celebrity Get Me Out Of Here* during a sequence where Mike Read attempted to pull Jenni Bond out of a whirlpool of moths.

The panel were so impressed by both the sentiment and the skill in

TEXTCLUSIVE

Danielle's message - "BROCK-IT IS SO FIT. KERY 2 WIN" – that showbusiness insiders claim the rivals for the prize never stood a chance. Julian Malteser, a new media manager from Redditch, whose "DON'T WORRY ABOUT DINNER – THIS TRAINS TAKING FOREVER" was hotly tipped in the run up to the awards,

Danielle *(right)* whose message *(above)* wowed the judges, and *(above)* the message sent by Danielle *(right)* that wowed the judges *(not shown)*.

failed to even show up for the event, leaving red-faced organisers to promise that

next year's contest would be less of a one horse race.

CEREMONY

Danielle celebrated her victory by glancing briefly up at the podium from her table and texting "THX!!!!" to the panel using the "Send To Many" option. Lord Attenborough responded immediately with "GR8" and Colin Welland sent a smiley face made out of brackets.

RICHARD BRANSON

COO! THERE'S A BUNCH OF PRESS PHOTOGRAPHERS OUTSIDE

RICHARD BRANSON

I MUST RUSH OUT THERE WAVING AND GRINNING AT THE CAMERAS LIKE A LOON.

DRAT! THEY'RE ONLY INTERESTED IN PHOTOGRAPHING THE BECKHAMS NEXT DOOR.

OVER HERE, DAVID!

SNAP FLASH

POSH 'N' BECKS

WHAT WILL YOU BE DOING WITH THE GRASS CUTTINGS MR B?

THIS WILL TURN THEIR CAMERAS ON ME

I'LL LIE ON THIS BED OF NAILS WHILE AN ELEPHANT STANDS ON ME, IN ORDER TO PUBLICISE MY VIRGIN TRAIN SERVICE.

ERK! OW! YOW! THE PAIN IS EXCRUCIATING ~ BUT IT'LL BE WORTH IT FOR THE NEWSPAPER HEADLINE...

"BRANSON'S PRICKLE! VIRGIN BOSS IN ELEPHANT-ASTIC BED OF NAILS STUNT!"

WHAT A NICE ELEPHANT ~ I'LL GIVE IT A BUN

SNAP CLICK! FLASH

EH?

AND

BAH!

the GUARDIAN

BOLD SPICE

DARING VICTORIA GIVES TEACAKE TO TUSKER

NO MATTER ~ THIS WILL MAKE A GREAT PHOTO OPPORTUNITY

IN ORDER TO RAISE PUBLICITY FOR MY VIRGIN MEGASTORES, I'M GOING TO TAKE A BATH ~ IN MY OWN SHIT!

GAG! RETCH! WHAT AN APPALLING STENCH! BUT JUST THINK OF THE HEADLINE...

"RICHARD THE TURD! BILLIONAIRE BIGWIG BRANSON BATHES IN BUMPOO!"

TSK! WHERE DID ALL THESE FLIES COME FROM?

SWIPE

SNAP

FLASH

CLICK

COH!

The Economist

SWAT A NUISANCE

POSH AND BECKS HARRASSED BY WINGED INSECT

AT LAST ~ THE BECKHAMS ARE GOING INDOORS

NOW'S MY CHANCE TO GRAB THE HEADLINES

I'LL WIND MYSELF THROUGH THIS GIANT MANGLE TO DRUM UP PUBLICITY FOR VIRGIN ATLANTIC AIRWAYS

OOYAH! GASP! I CAN SEE THE HEADLINE NOW...

WIND WIND

"WRING OUT THE BRANSON! VIRGIN SUPREMO GOES FLAT OUT FOR AIRLINE!"

POP!

OOPS!

THE MANGLE'S SQUEEZED MY TEETH OUT!

WHEEEEE CHOMP!

FLUTTER

CLICK FLASH PAPARATZ

GRR!

INTERNATIONAL HERALD TRIBUNE

UNBE-LEAF-ABLE

TREE SHEDS DETRITUS ON BECKINGHAM PALACE LAWN

THAT DOES IT! I GIVE UP!

HUNH? WHAT'S GOING ON NEXT DOOR?

HOORAY! THE BECKHAMS ARE MOVING HOUSE TO GET SOME PRIVACY FROM THE PAPARAZZIS

HOUSE SOLD

NOW THE PHOTOGRAPHERS WILL BE INTERESTED IN ME INSTEAD

SHORTLY- VROOM

LOOKS LIKE SOMEONE'S MOVING IN NEXT DOOR ALREADY

HOUSE SOLD

I WONDER WHO IT IS

TAPPITY TAPPITY

OH NO! IT'S ABI TITMUSS'S KNOCKERS!

SNAP CLICK FLASH

BIG SMILE OVER HERE, MISS TITMUSS'S KNOCKERS!

BOUNCE

Letterbocks

HOW come rap artist *Dr. Dre* can use the 'N' word on his multi-million selling albums and win a MOBO award, yet when I used it at my son's football match I was asked to leave the park? Once again, it's one law for the rich and another for the poor.

Reg Ashcroft
Bradford

APPARENTLY, people who can imagine things in 3 dimensions make very good molecular chemists. Well, I can imagine pushing my face right between Jordan's breasts until my head is completely enveloped by them. And get this... I'm emeritus Professor of Molecular Chemistry at Cambridge University.

Prof N. Tucker
Keys College, Camb.

I WOULD like to send a great big thank you to the viewers of BBC's *Crime Watch*. Whilst I was watching the other night I saw a re-enactment of a robbery I had done some weeks earlier. Nick Ross announced that a caller rang the programme to say he thought the stolen goods were in a warehouse, which indeed they were. Thanks to this tip off, I had time to go out and move the booty to another location just before the filth arrived. That's what I call public service broadcasting.

M Bibby
Manchester

YESTERDAY at work I spotted a lad who I used to bully in my class at school. Just for old time's sake, I followed him to the toilets, flushed his head down the pan and scattered the contents of his briefcase over the floor. True to form, the four eyed shitty pants ran straight back into the boardroom and told the managing director on me. Some people's lives just never move on, do they?

Tim Stent
e-mail

I'M sick and tired of women droning on and on about the pain of childbirth when they have access to any amount of pain relief. Where was the nurse with the gas and air or the epidural needle when Andrew Skelfington kicked me in the nuts with his big boots with Blakey's on in the school changing rooms in 1978?

D Jones
Wales

I AM a vicar and I was recently hauled over the coals by my bishop for doodling a penis in the margins of one of the bibles in my church. Yet the other day, I saw a stinkhorn fungus,

shaped like an erect penis, growing in the churchyard. Now I was taught at vicar school that God created everything on earth, so it would appear that he too has been doodling penises. The bishop should be bollocking God as well as me, but surprise, surprise, he doesn't. Once again, it's one law for omnipotent deities and another law for Joe Public.

Rev. J Public
Tadcaster

SO a cockroach can live for nine days after its head has been chopped off. It makes you wonder why they bother to have heads in the first place.

Julie Speedie
York

SO the Home Secretary plans to force us to carry identity cards with our iris patterns encoded onto them. That's rich. How dare David Blunkett judge people on their eyes when his don't even work. It would be like the head of the DVLC not having a number plate on his car.

T. Harris
Leeds

'ONE pound a week will supply water for an entire village in Tanzania', says Oxfam. So how come United Utilities charge me twenty pounds a month for my three bedroom semi? The fleecing bastards.

Tracey Cusick
Cumbria

THESE suicide bombers really get my goat. What an evil way to kill innocent people, running screaming into a crowded place like madmen, blowing themselves and everyone else to bits. Whatever happened to good old-fashioned gentlemen terrorists like the IRA, who'd quietly pop a nail bomb under a pub table and leave without making a song and dance about it.

Charles Nylon
London

MR Nylon (above letter) does not know what he is talking about. Gentlemen terrorists, indeed. When you get stang off a wasp, it just flies off to sting again and again in the style of the IRA bombers that Mr Nylon so admires. However, when a bee stings, it pulls its arse inside out and, like a suicide bomber, dies. And I think that we'd all agree that bees are much nicer than wasps.

Bamber Ross
Ross on Wye

I'M afraid Mr Ross's insect/terrorist analogy (above letter) doesn't hold water. The reason that we agree that bees are nicer than wasps is nothing at all to do with their stinging ability. It is because bees are furry, like little black and orange flying teddy bears that make jam. Wasps on the other hand are all hard and have them Darth Vader faces. And they chase you when you run off.

Prof J. Shiels
Dept of Entomology
Maudling College, Oxford

WHILE cleaning out the back of my fridge the other day, I found a half-full carton of 'fresh full-cream milk', but when I drank it I threw up and spent the rest of the week in bed. Fresh, my arse.

D Rimjob
e-mail

I READ in the paper that you can get AIDS off a mosquito. Well anyone sick enough to have bestial anal sex with an insect deserves everything they get in my opinion.

Sam McCrohan
Guildford

Lumley in New Leg Fear

THE WORLD of showbiz was rocked once again in the early hours of this morning as rumours that Joanna Lumley may have grown a third leg began to circulate.

It had earlier breathed a sigh of relief after speculation that she had possibly lost her left leg above the knee was scotched when she appeared at a hastily-convened press conference with two legs.

Baseless gossip about the 50-year-old *Ab Fab* star suggested that a freak third leg could have emerged from her lisk as a result of her perhaps accidentally drinking from a glass containing gamma radiation which might possibly have been left on a table at London's swanky Grosvenor House by an absent-minded scientist.

"If this proves to be correct then it will be a dark day for the world of entertainment," speculated her sombre co-star Jennifer Saunders.

"But Joanna's a real trouper. I'm sure her personal courage would enable her to easily overcome any obstacles that perhaps growing an extra leg might put in her path."

TELL US WHAT YOU THINK

How many legs has Joanna Lumley got? It's your chance to decide. Text the word LUMLEY, followed by the number of legs you think she's got, to 83125. Calls cost 25p, and we'll print your verdict in the next issue.

'SPIDERMAN! Spiderman! Does whatever a spider can!' So went the lyrics to the 70s cartoon. Does this include lying on his back lamely waving his shattered limbs in the air after being hit with a rolled up newspaper like the big, hairy bastard that just tried to run across my carpet?

M Perris
e-mail

I HATE watching *Dad's Army* with my gran - "he's dead', "Ooh, he's dead", "ooooh, he died very young". Morbid old bint.

Charlie Tetlow
e-mail

THE reason Britain lost so many planes during the war might be because they painted enormous targets on the side of them. Mind you, the nazis weren't much better – they had a sort of X on theirs.

Richard Low
Glasgow

MY barber makes me sick. If he really gave a toss what I was doing for my holiday, then he would recall from the last 6 times I've been in there that I'm not fucking having one this year.

Doug Candlish
North Shields

IT'S a shame that Lord Archer wasn't stripped of his peerage on his release from prison last year. It is some consolation, however, that he is now referred to as a 'disgraced peer'. It makes him the titled equivalent of a loved and trusted dog that has shat on the living room carpet. I hope he spends all day in the Upper House looking at his shoes.

S Thorn
Hexham

'YOU can't compare apples with pears', so the saying goes. Really? Well one is nice to eat and useful in cooking, the other is horribly gritty and either soft as shit or hard as knockers. That's that put to bed.

Andre Formica
e-mail

FOLLOWING the letter from G. Gladstone of Newcastle (letters page 51) regarding a small bus he had seen recently. I saw this little bin lorry recently. If anyone has seen a smaller bin lorry recently I'll eat Mr. Gladstone's hat too.

N Weller
Surrey

A RECENT TV documentary described deafness as 'the Invisible Disability'. This is surely the fault of hearing aid manufacturers who have made their products smaller and smaller over the years. Indeed, many now fit completely inside the ear. A return to large, conspicuous hearing aids is surely the answer. Better still, a large ear trumpet would alert everyone to the fact that very loud and slow shouting is called for.

M Jeff
e-mail

THE NSPCC keeps going on TV and saying that unless I send them three quid a month, a baby called William won't be so lucky next time. I suggest that we don't give in to these extortionists and blackmailers, or they'll be back with a threat to top him if we don't send them a fiver.

Tracey Cusick,
Cumbria

HALITOSIS sufferers. Try to regulate your breathing so that you breathe out when everybody else does.
Rob Ireland, Manchester

MEN. Can't get a blow job? Simply strip bollock naked, plonk yourself arse-first into an empty dustbin, and you should be able to do it yourself. Use a pile of tyres instead of a dustbin if you require deep throat.
Allen Bethell, e-mail

LADIES! Putting your mouth and chin inside a pint glass and sucking hard for three minutes is an excellent way to give yourself a 'Fred Flintstone' five o'clock shadow.
Michelle Armsponder, Port Sunlight

WHITE wine splashed onto a red wine stain will clean it up quickly. Similarly, fat splashes on clothes can be easily removed by rubbing salad onto the affected area.
Rick Stein, Padstow

MEN. Re-create the excitement of a Soho peep show by going to a nudist beach wearing a burka.
J. Geils, Band

COUCH potatoes. When eating Pringles, conserve energy by removing them from the tube two at a time but only taking half a bite. Hey Pesto! You are eating the same amount of Pringles for only half of the arm movements.
Wooly, Seaham

BUSY executives. Don't buy a Dachshund. Their amusing sausage shape means they take 50% longer to stroke than other dogs, and time is money.
R Bowen, e-mail

GENTS. Save yourself embarrassment on washday. Place a strip of 1-inch wide sellotape in the gusset of your underpants every morning. This can simply be wiped clean after any unfortunate accidents.
Kenny, Fife

ONE ARMED men. If your partner is thinking about getting breast implants, convince her to save money and only get one done.
Sam McCrohan, Guildford

GIVE house spiders a taste of their own medicine by applying a coat of spray mount to all the surfaces in your home.
Felixthehat, e-mail

PARENTS. A small amount of cement added to your child's sandcastle will ensure that his/her hard work is not ruined when the tide comes in.
Corp. Rock & Sgt. Roll, e-mail

'SPEAK Your Mind on Radio 5', say the adverts. Well, everytime I've tried, I got as far as "I think Nicky Campbell is a fucking tw..." and they cut me off.

Nick Duffy
Preston

I WAS watching the News recently and I saw David Blunkett meet some bloke in a car park then walk into a building holding his hand whilst a load of on-lookers stood around clapping. Hats off to the Home Secretary for being so openly gay in today's narrow minded society.

James Watson
e-mail

On the subject of David Blunkett, there has been much speculation in the press recently as to his suitability to be a minister. He doesn't seem to like the job very much, as everytime I see him on television, he's not working but taking his dog for a walk.

Peter Dayson-Smith
e-mail

I WAS lying in bed the other night when my girlfriend, Tracey Peacock, farted on my leg in her sleep. I don't know whether or not I should say anything to her, as I don't want to cause her any embarassment. What would other *Viz* readers do in this situation?

John Stewart
Northants

BEFORE animal rights activists complaint about elephants being forced to dance and do tricks at the circus, they should spare a thought for the ones wandering the plains of Africa bored shitless because they've got nothing to do.

Nathan Geary
e-mail

I PUT a pound coin into the slot meter on a trolley at Morrison's today and nothing happened. At least on a fruit machine you get some flashing lights for wasting your money. No wonder Ken Morrison is a millionaire with scams like this.

Teddy Raffle
e-mail

soap dish
with Jo Soap

MADCAP comedy legend **Sir Norman Wisdom** is dusting down his trademark flat cap for a new lease of life in Coronation Street.

The 89-year-old is set to appear in Weatherfield in a hilarious cameo appearence.

He is the latest comic to star in the Street, following Peter Kay's unfuny one-off as drayman Eric Gartside and Roy Hudd's irritating appearances as undertaker Archie Shuttleworth.

Sir Norman will play pensioner Ernie Crabbe, who breaks his hip in a fall outside the Rovers return and later dies alone from the MRSA superbug in a filthy NHS hospital.

Sir Norman, who was knighted in 2000 told reporters last night: "I'm thrilled to bits to be on Coronation Street. It's a national institution and I'm really looking forward to playing the archetypal cheeky chappie with a glint in his eye who takes a tumble and dies a horrible lonely death without any friends or relatives to comfort him."

Fears for 'Overworked PM'

THERE were mounting concerns for Tony Blair's health last night, after colleagues admitted that the PM is 'in danger of becoming overworked.'

Rumours that Blair has too much on his plate started to circulate after he was spotted presenting BBC News24 every morning between 4am and 5am, when no-one is watching.

van

A nervous Downing Street spokesman confirmed that the exhausted PM was also driving a van for Mastercare on Mondays and Wednesdays.

betty

But, as if that wasn't enough for an already bleary-eyed Blair, every Thursday he mans the tills at the Barton Edge

Blair enjoys a rare moment of relaxation with with Ann Clwyd in the House of Commons bar yesterday

Watermill Experience, where members of the re-enactment team describe him as 'courteous and friendly, but clearly very tired.'

The latest revelations about the PM's frantic workload follow an embarrassing blunder this week when Blair had to cancel a meeting with Kofi Annan because it was the first Sunday of the month, when he runs his stall at Merton Abbey Mills craft fair selling some of the jewellery he makes in his precious spare time.

Home Secretary Jack Straw, who looks almost human without his spectacles, has called for the Prime Minister's salary to be increased to at least £13,000pa to cover the shortfall, should he be forced to give up his jobs on the side.

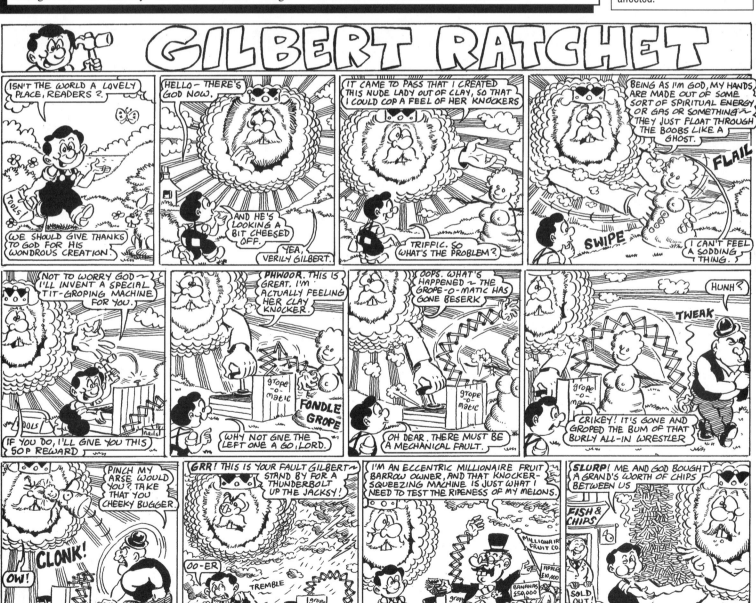

Will We Ever Know

IT WAS THE ROYAL DEATH that shocked the nation. On December 22nd 2003, the country woke up to the news that Pharos, the Queen's favourite corgi, had been savaged to death by one of Princess Anne's pitbull terriers. Its back legs brutally ripped off by the beast, the plucky dog fought back bravely against its attacker, but stood little chance.

Six weeks later, there has still been no official investigation into the tragedy. And as public dismay continues to mount, the authorities seem no closer to finding out the truth of what actually happened on that fateful day.

Official reports maintain that the Queen's favourite pooch's hind legs were chewed off by terrier Florence during the vicious Christmas attack at Sandringham. But many observers believe that the finger of suspicion points elsewhere.

secret

Former Palace dog-handler Douglas Milburn told us: "It's an open secret that Pharos was murdered by

By our Royal Correspondent
Aiken Drum
the Man in the Moon

Dottie, not Florence as has been claimed in the papers. Florence was nowhere near that corgi, and I can prove it."

door

According to Milburn, affectionately known in royal circles as "Dogshit Duggie" until he was dismissed on Boxing Day, the innocent Florence is being set up as a 'patsy'. He said: "The real villain in all this is Dottie, yet she's getting off scot free. I know Florence didn't kill Pharos because I was worming her in the kitchen when the attack happened."

Now, in a bid to prevent a

Killer English Bull terrier Dottie, yesterday and its victim Pharos (left). Inset, Princess Anne with a face like a slapped arse.

miscarriage of justice, Dogshit Duggie has come out from under the stairs to dish the dogdirt on Dottie.

"That dog's a bad one, make no mistake. She's hit the headlines two or three times for attacking children and housemaids, but a lot of her other crimes have been hushed up.

"For instance, one morning I was devilling some Pedigree Chum for the royal dogs' breakfasts when I heard a blood-curdling scream from the hall. I rushed out to find Dottie lying on the mat, eating the postman's arm.

"I thought it might be possible for a doctor to re-attach the arm, but Dottie wouldn't let go of her prize. She growled if anyone went near her.

"In the end, the Queen came down to see what all the fuss was. She gave the postman £50 and an OBE on condition that he never told anybody what had happened. He had lost a lot of blood, so he wasn't thinking straight and agreed.

sandwich

"Another time, Princess Anne was visiting a cat res-

Where Were You?

EVERYONE remembers where they were when they heard the tragic news that Pharos, the Queen's favourite corgi, had been killed. We asked five C-list celebrities and a recently relegated D-list celebrity to recall what *they* were doing when the shocking news broke.

BBC Baghdad Correspondent *Raggy Omaar*

"*I REMEMBER* I was recording a piece about a suicide bombing at a Baghdad hospital when the first reports about Pharos's death bega to trickle across the wires. The news seemed so shocking and at first I didn't want to believe it. Later I just wandered the streets for hours and hours, desperately trying to make some sort of sense out of the tragedy. I suppose I was in a in a state of shock. I think we all were."

Entertainers *Keith Harris* and *Orville the Duck*

"*WE* were about to go on stage in our pantomime at Crewe Theatre Royal when we heard what had happened on the radio. Orville was so upset he wanted to cancel the show, but I told him he had to go on. 'But I can't', I kept making him repeat. In the end, we went on but the audience was very subdued. I've never got so few laughs in a show, and coming from me that's saying something."

Flamboyant Airport star *Jeremy Spake*

"*I WAS* about to tuck into several pies when my neighbour came in and told me the news. I was so upset I lost all my appetite and had to force the pies down. When I had finished them I could barely face my pudding of six mocha and almond bombs. But I did. I think it's what Pharos would have wanted."

Cheeky TV God-Botherer *Nick Hancock*

"*I WAS* watching TV when the programme was interrupted with a newsflash. Such terrible events can lead one to question one's faith. How can a lovely corgi like Pharos have his life cut short, whilst wicked animals such as wasps, piranha fish and crocodiles are allowed to live? All we can do is trust God in his wisdom. It is all part of the Lord's plan. Hallelujah. Praise Him. **Praaaaaise Him.**"

Renault Car salesman *Thierry Henry*

"*WE* were training at Highbury when Arson called us into the dressing room to break the news. Some of the lads broke down. They couldn't believe Pharos had gone, and they'd never see him being carried down the steps of the Queen's plane any more. It brought back to me vividly the feeling of loss felt by the whole French nation in 1973 when Giscard d'Estang's hamster Bertrand choked to death after over-stuffing its cheeks with sunflower seeds."

Most Haunted Medium *Derek Acorah*

"*I FOUND* out about about Pharos's death before anyone else. I was having a cup of tea with Yvette Fielding when my spirit guide Sam walked through the wall and told me there was a ghost corgi humping his leg. Yvette screamed. I asked Sam to look at the collar to see if it had an address. When he told me it read 'Pharos, Buckingham Palace' I went cold and Yvette screamed again."

the Truth?
Royal Death still Shrouded in Mystery

Yappier times ~ Pharos (above, left in photo) a few days before the attack and (right) being carried onto a plane yesterday.

cue centre. Her advisers had suggested it might be a bad idea to take her dog with her, but as usual she refused to listen.

"After cutting the ribbon, Anne was shown a basket of abandoned two-week-old kittens which had just been rescued. Without warning, and in front of over 100 specially-invited guests, Dottie tore into them, ripping them limb from limb. There was blood and cat fur everywhere. It was like an explosion at a gonk factory.

sesame

"Needless to say, Princess Anne didn't make the slightest attempt to stop the attack. The crowd were left to stand around, smiling awkwardly and making polite smalltalk while the carnage unfolded in front of them.

"If word of that terrible attack had leaked out it would have been curtains for Dottie.

But as usual, the Royal family managed to hush things up by giving everyone present £50 and making them all Knights Commander of the Order of the Garter."

But it's not just postmen and kittens who have found themselves on the wrong side of the Princess's dog. According to Duggie, one very senior member of the Royal family once felt the might of the pitbull's mighty jaws.

hot cross

"I remember on one occasion, the entire Royal family had gone for a picnic in the grounds of Balmoral Castle. I was present in my offical capacity to shovel up any dirts left by Princess Anne's dogs.

"Everything was going swimmingly. The family were letting their hair down, throwing frisbees and playing games. When I heard the Queen Mum screaming I thought she was having a fun fight with one of the Princes. When I saw what was actually going on, my blood froze.

Unseen by the rest of the party, Dottie's hunting instincts had come to the fore. She had sensed that the

Queen Mum was the oldest and weakest person present, and had separated her from the rest of the group before launching a deadly attack.

By the time I got to her, the dog had bitten one of her hips off.

buttered

The Queen Mum was rushed to hospital by air ambulance to have a new hip fitted. Meanwhile Princess Anne just said, "bad girl," and tapped Dottie gently on the nose with a rolled-up newspaper.

I knew at that moment that Dottie would kill again. I just prayed that next time it would be a small child or a housemaid and not one of the Queen's beloved corgis. Alas, as we now know, my prayer went unanswered."

tapped

A Palace spokesman refused to comment on the allegations, but confirmed that Milburn had been employed by the Royal family as a dog

handler. He told us: "Douglas Milburn was dismissed on December 26th following an investigation into the theft of a quantity of underwear from the Duchess of Wessex's quarters at Buckingham palace."

Duggie told us: "The Royal family has set me up. I'm a patsy, just like Florence. The Queen offered to buy my silence by giving me £50 and making me the Marquess of Cornwall, but I told them where to stick it. The next day when I was searched on my way out of the Palace and found to be wearing four pairs of Sophie Rhys-Jones's used scanties, I knew that somebody had planted them in my trousers."

At Hammersmith Magistrates yesterday Douglas Milburn pleaded guilty to 4 counts of theft, and asked for 208 similar cases to be taken into consideration. Sentencing was deferred until March, pending psychiatric reports.

Princess Diana ~ Didn't live to see this happen.

Pharos Fact File

Name: *Pharos*
Position amongst Queen's corgis: *Favourite*
Breed: *Corgi*
Colour: *Corgi colour*
Age: *Between 10 and 20*
Age in dog years: *Between 70 and 140*
Favourite food: *Dog food*
Sex: *Unknown*
Fave group: *Busted*
Likes: *Walking, barking, sniffing other dogs up the arse, being carried off planes, shitting*
Dislikes: *Cats, fireworks*
Colour Vision: *None*
Black & White Vision: *Yes*
Sense of Smell: *Keen*
No. of legs before attack: *4*
No. of legs after attack: *2*
Existent state before attack: *Alive*
Existent state after attack: *Dead*

PHAROS was the dog the nation had grown to love. With its waggy tail, cheerful yapping and wet nose it was to all of us the Queen's Dog of Hearts. As a tribute to his memory, here is a moving Fact File to cut out and treasure.

Rude kid...

HAVE YOU BEEN A GOOD LITTLE BOY THIS YEAR?

UP YER ARSE CUNTY CHOPS!

Six times table crashes

THE GOVERNMENT was last night planning emergency measures to re-nationalise the six times table, after its value dramatically plummeted.

The crash followed the news that the troubled owner of the times table, the private consortium Six.com, had gone into receivership.

As the Treasury and the London Stock Exchange appealed for calm, there was panic buying of eggs and dice. At Lord's, the England cricket team walked off the pitch in disgust after skipper Michael Vaughan knocked one into the crowd that was only worth five runs.

SIX

By yesterday lunchtime, two sixes were no longer twelve but nine, and at 2.45pm the Chancellor, making a statement in Parliament, announced an emergency six times table.

"With immediate effect, 6x1=2, 6x2=4 and 6x3=6," he told a packed and rowdy House of Commons. He went on to say that an hour would now last 20 minutes, but confirmed that for the time being, a week would remain seven days long.

BROWN: knocked for six.

But mahogany-tinted Europhobe Robert Kilroy was hopping bonkers at the news. "This is exactly why we should withdraw from the EU," he foamed, while assistants behind him operated the levers that control his face.

How the emergency table will affect YOU

WINNERS

DOMINO MANUFACTURERS save 66% paint costs on double sixes

SCHOOLBOYS six of the best now over in just two strokes

NESTLÉ Profits treble on sales of 'Bar Six' biscuits

LOSERS

INSECTS – must learn to walk on 2 legs like everyone else

PETER ANDRE – famous six-pack now slashed to just two muscles

THE DEVIL – the number of the beast devalued by 2/3

CHRIST, WHAT A STINK!

R.H. '04

Arise, Sir Midge?

Band Aid Ure still clinging to knighthood dream ~claim

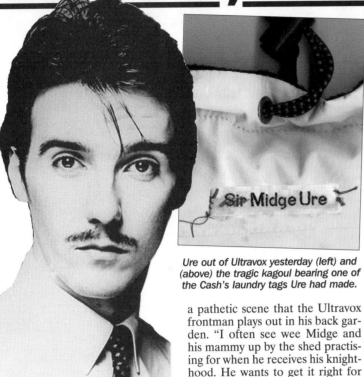

Ure out of Ultravox yesterday (left) and (above) the tragic kagoul bearing one of the Cash's laundry tags Ure had made.

IT'S TWENTY YEARS to the day since Band Aid hit the charts with their record-breaking single *'Do They Know it's Christmas?'*. Since then, the pop song has raised countless millions of pounds for starving people all around the world. Ten years after the song hit the charts, Bob Geldof was given his thanks in the form of an Honorary Knighthood from the Queen. But a further decade on, his co-writer is still waiting for his letter from the palace to drop on the mat.

But friends of Midge Ure, the mild-mannered Scotsman who penned the song with Sir Bob, say that he has not given up hope of being knighted.

sorrow

Mrs Morag Crabtree, who lives next door to Ure's modest semi-detached house in Auchtermuchty, Fife, spoke last night of her sorrow that Midge has been snubbed. "I feel so sorry for the wee man," she told reporters. "Every morning I hear the patter of his little feet scurrying down the stairs to check the post. Then, I hear a deep sigh, and him slowly trudging back to his room. It's heartbreaking."

Morag is also regularly witness to

a pathetic scene that the Ultravox frontman plays out in his back garden. "I often see wee Midge and his mammy up by the shed practising for when he receives his knighthood. He wants to get it right for the big day, if it ever comes," she told us. "He kneels down in front of her and she taps him three times on the shoulders with a breadknife and says 'Arise, Sir Midge'. He looks so proud in his suit and his little top hat, I could weep for the man, I really could."

let's dance

But perhaps the saddest evidence of Midge's disappointment came to light when Mrs Crabtree was planning a walk in the Highlands. "I went round next door to see if I could borrow a kagoul for my trip.

Mrs Ure handed me one of Midge's and told me that I could keep it as he had recently grown out of it," she told us. "When I looked in the collar, I saw he had a Cash's laundry label in it that read 'Sir Midge Ure', and the 'Sir' had been scribbled out in biro. He must have had a batch of them made when Bob Geldof got his knight-

Scruffy bleeder Sir Bob, yesterday

hood. The poor mite must have thought he was next, bless him. Och, it was pitiful."

china girl

Although he has never spoken publicly about it, it is belived that Ure, 48, feels agrieved that the four-letter mouthed Boomtown Rat has received more credit for the charity single than himself. And with good reason, according to pop scientist Dr Dave Kidderminster-Jenson. "It's well known that Sir Bob wrote the words to *'Do They Know it's Christmas?'*, whilst Midge done the tune," he told us. "But my research has shown that had the song been released as a poem without any music, it would scarcely have dented the top 100. I am certain that Midge's contribution to the single is responsible for 99% of the money raised. It's a travesty that he hasn't been knighted."

ch-ch-ch-ch changes

A spokesman for Buckingham Palace told us: "It's nothing personal against Mr Ure. It's just that Her Majesty does the knighthoods alphabetically, and she's usually used them all up by about R or S. That's why Donald Sinden had to wait so long.

" If Midge Ure changes his name to perhaps Midge Aardvark, or Midge Abacus, he'll probably get one in the New Year's Honours," he added.

What's URE Opinion?

'Do They Know it's Christmas?' raised untold millions to alleviate famine in Africa. (It has only recently been out-charitied by Elton John's Candle in the Wind, Lady Di re-mix which made a billion pounds to pay for a beautiful algae-filled trench in Hyde Park and a moving court case against Franklin Mint).

But is it enough to earn its writer a Knighthood?

We went on the street to do an Ultravox-pop of the ordinary Britiash public. Should Midge be made Sir Midge, or should he be condemmned to stay plain Mr Ure? Here's what **YOU** said:

"...Bob Geldoff is very scruffy, and by his own admission only has one bath a week. And yet he is knighted. Midge Ure on the other hand, who is always immaculately turned out, remains a commoner. There is no justice in this world."
J Wells, Derby

"...forget about Band Aid. Midge Ure has one of the neatest moustaches I have ever seen. Along with his geometrically trimmed sideburns, I think he should receive a knighthood for services to facial hair."
M Hartstone, Leeds

"...undoubtedly he has done a lot for

the starving millions in the third world. But let's not forget that he is only 5 foot 4 tall. Dubbing him a knight would make this country a laughing stock. Who next?... Sir Ronnie Corbett? Sir Mini-me? Sir him out of Diff'rent Strokes?"
B Riddell, Bolton

"...a knighthood is insufficient reward for what Ure has done for charity. I think he should be made a life peer."
J Townshend, Luton

"... a life peerage would be a slap in the face after all Ure has done to alleviate poverty around the globe. I think he

should be crowned King Midge I of England."
L Stonehouse, Hull

"...I think Ure had ulterior motives in his raising millions for charity. Call me cynical, but I think it is no co-incidence that just five years after Band Aid, If I Was made number 12 in the charts. How high would it have reached had he not been involved in the charity?"
B Pollard, Leeds

"...Ure has wasted little time cynically cashing in on his Band Aid fame by releasing Band Aid 20 this year. He should be publically hung - and I'll pull the lever!"
Albert Pierrepoint, London

ELTON JOHN'S BACCY RUN

ELTON IS RETURNING FROM A CONCERT TOUR OF EUROPE IN HIS SOLID GOLD JET PLANE

HEATHROW

WELCOME TO BRITAIN

ELTON - 1

WELL SIR ELTON, I THINK YOUR EUROPEAN TOUR WAS A GREAT SUCCESS.

IT CERTAINLY WAS! WHILE WE WERE IN FRANCE I BOUGHT 200 PACKS OF OLD HOLBORN TO SELL DOWN THE PUB BACK HOME

IF I FLOG THEM FOR £3·50 A TIME, I COULD MAKE UP TO A HUNDRED QUID CLEAR PROFIT.

THE PROBLEM IS ~ HOW AM I GOING TO SMUGGLE ALL THIS BACCY THROUGH CUSTOMS?

HEH HEH! I'VE STASHED IT IN THE HOLLOW SOLES OF MY GIGANTIC PLATFORM BOOTS.

NOW TO CASUALLY SAUNTER PAST THE CUSTOMS OFFICIALS

NO SMOKING

SORRY, SIR ELTON ~ YOU'RE TOO TALL TO FIT THROUGH THE METAL DETECTOR

HERE ~ LET ME HELP YOU OFF WITH THOSE BOOTS

HUNH?

NO! I'VE, ER, JUST REMEMBERED, I'VE LEFT SOMETHING ON THE PLANE

PHEW! THAT WAS A CLOSE SHAVE. I'LL HAVE TO RESORT TO PLAN 'B'

AND FOR THAT, I'LL NEED THIS LONG LENGTH OF WIRE AND SOME STRING

HO HO! HOW DO YOU LIKE THESE GIANT SPECTACLE FRAMES I'VE CONSTRUCTED?

SUCH IS MY REPUTATION FOR FLAMBOYANCE AND ECCENTRICITY, NO-ONE WILL SUSPECT THEY'RE ACTUALLY MADE OUT OF PACKETS OF HOOKY SNOUT.

BAGGAGE CAROUSEL

UNFORTUNATELY, I CAN'T SEE A BLINKING THING THROUGH THEM

CUSTOMS

HOPE I'M GOING IN THE RIGHT DIRECTION

CAROUSEL

WAH!

TRIP!

SHORTLY

NEVER MIND, I'VE ANOTHER IDEA

SHAKE SHAKE

FIRST I'LL NEED TO EMPTY ALL THE TOBACCO OUT OF THE POUCHES...

AND HEY PRESTO! A TEN KG OLD HOLBORN HAIRPIECE

THE CUSTOMS OFFICIAL WON'T DARE PASS COMMENT ON THIS WIG, FOR FEAR THAT I MIGHT FLY INTO A HUFFY TANTRUM.

NO SMOKING

AFTERNOON, BERT. I'VE JUST GOT TO DO A SPOT OF WELDING ON THIS METAL BARRIER.

RIGHTO ALF

YIKES! THE SPARKS OFF THAT WELDER'S TORCH HAVE SET FIRE TO MY BACCY BARNET.

SNIFF SNIFF! I CAN SMELL TOBACCO SMOKE ~ WHO'S HAVING A CRAFTY ROLL-UP?

TIME TO BEAT A HASTY RETREAT

THIS CAN'T FAIL. I'LL PUSH A PIANO THROUGH CUSTOMS WHILE PLAYING MY TRIBUTE SONG TO PRINCESS DIANA

EVERYONE WILL BE SO OVERWHELMED WITH EMOTION, THEY WON'T NOTICE THE 200 PACKETS OF THROATBURN HIDDEN UNDER THE LID.

EXIT EXIT

GOODBYE, LADY DI YOU WERE NICE AS PIE..

PLINKETTY PLONK

TRUNDLE

LIKE A ROSE WITHOUT GREENFLY OH WHY DID YOU HAVE TO DIE?

SCAMPER

> SOB < IT'S SO SAD

> PARP! < TRULY SHE WAS THE PRINCESS OF HEARTS

EXIT EXIT

ARF ARF! I'M HOME FREE

THE DOG AND BASTARD

BAR

NOW TO FLOG MY BACCY DOWN THE PUB. AND AT £3·50 A PUNT, I'LL SOON BE RICH!

OH NO! ROD STEWART HAS MUSCLED IN ON MY PATCH ~ AND HE'S SELLING HIS BACCY FOR £3·25!

HA HA (CROAK). I SMUGGLED 200 PACKS OF GOLDEN VIRGINIA BACK FROM GREECE IN MY BIG STICKY-OUT ARSE!

78

...HERE WE ARE, DOLLY.

SPESS XPRESS

FREE EYE TEST!! YOUR GLASSES IN 1 HOUR 7 TO 14 DAYS GUARANTEED!

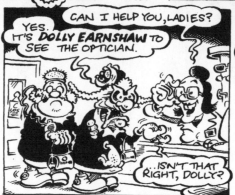

CAN I HELP YOU, LADIES?

YES. IT'S DOLLY EARNSHAW TO SEE THE OPTICIAN.

...ISN'T THAT RIGHT, DOLLY?

I SAID, ISN'T THAT RIGHT, DOLLY.

HOLD ON ADA. I CAN'T HEAR. I'LL HAVE TO TURN ME POP-IT UP.

WHEEEEE·OOOOO OOOOO·EEEEEEE...!

WHEEEEE!!

THERE. NOW. WHAT DID YOU SAY, ADA?

I SAID, YOU'VE COME TO SEE MR. GARRITY, HAVEN'T YOU?

CHARITY?! WHAT CHARITY? I'M NOT GIVING OWT TO THE BLACKS.

ERM...MR. GARRITY RETIRED TWENTY YEARS AGO.

...BUT IF YOU'D LIKE TO POP THROUGH TO THE EXAMINATION ROOM, MR. McFERGUS WILL SEE YOU.

OOH McFERGUS. HE SOUNDS NICE. I LIKE THE SOUND OF HIM.

AYE. NICE AND CLEAN HE SOUNDS.

VERY CLEAN, YES.

AH- GOOD MORNING, LADIES. NOW, WHICH ONE'S MRS. EARNSHAW?

I AM.

NO YOU'RE NOT, ADA. I AM. I'M DOLLY EARNSHAW. I'M ALMOST CERTAIN OF IT.

OOH NO... YOU'RE NOT DOLLY, DOLLY. FOR A START, DOLLY'S GOT GLASSES LIKE MINE AND...

...NO...NOW...HOLD YOUR HORSES... YOU'RE RIGHT. YOU ARE DOLLY... 'CAUSE YOU WERE MARRIED TO HECTOR WHO HAD THAT STROKE, WEREN'T YOU...

EEH... WAS I?

YES. YOU KNOW. HECTOR. HE WORKED IN THAT CHIP SHOP.

HECTOR... HECTOR... NO....

YOU MUST BE THINKING OF SOMEONE ELSE, ADA. HAPPEN YOU ARE ME AFTER ALL.

NO I'M NOT, DOLLY. YOU REMEMBER THAT CHIP SHOP WHERE CISSIE GOT HAIR IN HER FISH CAKE ONCE.

HECTOR... HECTOR...

RUDDY GREAT LONG BLONDE ONE IT WERE.

...HECTOR...HECTOR...WHAT WERE HIS SECOND NAME AGAIN, ADA?

EARNSHAW, DOLLY. SAME AS YOURS.

YOU CREMATED HIM YESTERDAY, REMEMBER?

OH HIM, HECTOR EARNSHAW. USED TO WORK IN A CHIP SHOP.

WAS HE MY HUSBAND?

AYE.

EEH. WELL I'LL GO TO THE FOOT OF OUR STAIRS. IT MUST BE ME THEN, ADA.

PLEASE TAKE A SEAT, MRS. EARNSHAW. NOW, ARE YOU EXPERIENCING ANY VISUAL PROBLEMS - OR ARE YOU JUST HERE FOR A GENERAL EYE TEST?

...TEST.

YES, THAT'S RIGHT.

WELL, SHE NEEDS HER LOOKERS AND HER SEE-ERS FOR LOOKING AT THINGS, AND WHEN SHE READS SHE NEEDS HER READERS, HER LOOKERS AND HER SEE-ERS.

AND SHE STILL CAN'T SEE OWT.

80

Botty Bungle Doc given Bums Rush

Gerald Burch in happier times with bending arm, and (inset) bungling doc Eating Charlesworth yesterday.

A Tyneside surgeon was last night suspended on full pay after a patient who was booked in for routine anal surgery had his elbow removed by mistake.

Gerald Birch, a 45 year-old professional accordianist awoke in North Tyneside General hospital to discover that the haemorrhoids which had plagued him for years were still there...*but that his perfectly healthy right elbow had been amputated.*

A clearly upset Mr Birch told reporters: "When I came round from the op, my piles were still throbbing like mad. I thought it was probably stitches from the surgery. But then I realised that my right arm was stiff, and four inches shorter than the left." he asked a nurse what was going on, and was told that there must have been a mix up in the operating theatre.

CROSSHEAD

Bungling proctological surgeon, Dr Farnley Eating-Charlesworth who performed the operation later visited the ward to apologise in person to Mr Birch.

"He told me that it was an easy mistake to make, and not to worry because elbows usually grow back in a few months", said Birch from his home in Bedlington.

CROSSHEAD

"I hope it does, because at the minute my life is ruined. I can't bend my arm at all, and my hobbies are line dancing, darts and weight-lifting. And doing press-ups. They're not going to get away with this. I'm going for compensation."

Last night, a spokeman for the North Tyneside Hospital Trust issued a prepared statement: 'Dr Eating-Charlesworth has worked at North Tyneside General hospital for twenty years, and this is the first time he has confused a patient's rectum with their elbow. He has agreed to take leave and will remain away while a full investigation is carried out.

Mr Birch later phoned reporters to add that he also liked doing monkey impressions and winding buckets up from wells.

Can *YOU* tell your... ARSE from your ELBOW?

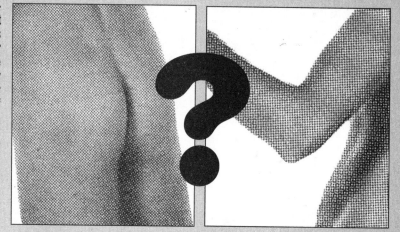

Despite skyscraping GCSE and A-Level results, surveys show that a shocking 60% of school leavers still can't tell their arse from their elbow, and the consequences are clear to see every time you try to buy some batteries from one of the junior staff at Dixons. The Department of Education has bowed to pressure and will introduce a stringent new Arse/Elbow Distinction Paper as part of the new GCSE syllabus next year, but what about the rest of us? You might think you know better, but do you? Try our fun quiz, and see if YOU can tell your arse from your elbow...

1. An hour after a satisfying casserole, you need to go to the lavatory for a number two. You've locked yourself in the bathroom, folded over the right page of Exchange and Mart, and made sure there's plenty of toilet roll. You're fully prepared. But what do you do next?

  a. *pull down your trousers, settle down on the toilet seat and dump your load*

  b. *roll up your sleeves, dip the crook of your arm into the bowl and shit your pants*

2. While attempting to shift a particularly stubborn stain from the ceramic hob of your cooker, you realise the job would be easier if you could use a little more of which substance?

  a. *Elbow grease*

  b. *Arse grease*

3. In an effort to spice up your love life, your partner offers to take you "up the arse" using whatever they have to hand. What do you do?

  a. *bury your face in the pillow and present your rear end to them like a bike rack*

  b. *stand in an 'I'm a little teapot' pose and beckon them into the crook of your arm*

4. While stirring some soup on the stove, you accidentally sit in the saucepan. You feel a scalding sensation somewhere between your spine and your legs and call an ambulance to ask what to do next. Where would you tell the paramedics you are being burnt?

  a. *Your arse*

  b. *Your elbow*

5. On a coach trip to an all-male bonding session, such as a football match, you decide to liven up the tedium of motorway travel by making a saucy display out of the back window at the family in the car behind. What would you do?

  a. *drop your trousers and press your bare buttocks against the glass*

  b. *push the tip of your bent arm against the rear windscreen, pointing at it and laughing*

6. While driving through an area with poor radio reception, you are forced to tune into the strongest local signal, which is the Steve Wright afternoon show on Radio 2. It isn't long before you realise that Steve Wright is causing you a terrible pain. Where?

  a. *In the arse*

  b. *In the elbow*

HOW DID YOU DO?

Score 2000 points for every time you answered a. and 0 points for every time you answered b.

0-2000 ~ Oh, dear! You really can't tell your arse from your elbow. Like many school leavers you probably also have minimal onion knowledge and cannot distinguish between the buttered and unbuttered sides of bread.

2000-10000 ~ Though most of the time you can easily tell your rear end from a hole in the ground, you have a little more difficulty distinguishing it from the hinged joint at the midway point of your arm. But don't worry! Try doing the test again, and this time not getting as many questions wrong.

10000-12000 ~ Well done! You can certainly tell your arse from your elbow. Putting clothes on is a breeze, and you rarely make the mistake of falling asleep at a table with your head nestled in the crook of your arse. Whether it's sitting down or nudging someone out of the way, you know the right tool for the job. Your expertise is likely to lead to a high flying career in either underwear modelling or standing in door-ways with your hands on your hips.

No Sex Please... WE

FIREMEN

FIREMEN

Britain's firemen are set to strike again, but this time it's not over pay, conditions or working hours. It's over their declining pulling power!

Once the country's most highly-sexed job, fire-fighting has recently fallen from its traditional number one position in the rumpy-pumpy professions chart. And union bosses fear that if the slide continues unchecked, firemen could even slip out of the top ten altogether by the end of the decade.

SEX

According to a survey carried out by the government's official sex watchdog OffBang, fire-fighting has now dropped behind financial management in the turn-on stakes. According to sex ombudsman Baroness Warnock, the scent of money rather than the scent of danger is what gets today's women going.

She told us: "Back in the eighties, the hunky heroes of films like Towering Inferno, Backdraft and Trumpton got a lot of ladies hot under the collar. They were attracted by the combination of strength and tenderness in six-packed firemen who fearlessly stepped into burning buildings to rescue babies and puppies without a thought for their own safety."

However according to Warnock, today's uncertain economic climate means women are increasingly transferring their sexual longings to men in the financial services sector. "Saving money has replaced saving lives as the biggest turn-on for ladies. Financial advisers, with their ability to juggle figures and fill in complicated forms, now have women going weak at the knees left, right and centre. Firemen have most definitely had their chips as the country's favourite heart-throbs."

VIOLIN

But fire union leader Andy Gilchrist slammed the new chart and pledged that his members would stay out on strike until the situation was rectified. He told us: "No fireman likes taking industrial action, but we can't sit back and allow our traditional position as the country's sexiest profession to be eroded in this way. We will be refusing to attend emergency calls until Britain's women come to their senses and once again think firemen are the horniest thing on legs."

BRIEF

And he had harsh words for government plans to bring in army recruits in Green Goddesses to provide emergency cover. "When Britain's birds see spotty squaddies tripping over their hoses like the Keystone Cops, they'll realise how hunky us real firemen are."

However, Britain's women were last night refusing to back down. Spokeswoman Germaine Greer told us: "We ladies have had the wool pulled over our eyes for too long. Firemen are simply not that sexy any more. Sicknote out of London's Burning was positively ugly, and the rest of the crew on Blue Watch was just plain.

PANT

"Compare that lot to some of the hunks you get in the financial services sector, like sexy Howard Brown from the

1 (23) Financial Adviser	2 (1) Fireman	3 (2) Professional Footballer	4 (4) Dentist	5 (3) Painter & Decorator	6 (8) Racing Driver

(Last year's position in brackets)

Firemen AXED

THE DOWNTURN in firefighters's fortunes has had knock-on effects in other industries.

Strippogram agencies have reported drops of up to 86% in demand for cheeky fireman strippers. One boss told us: "I used to take 40 or 50 bookings a week for firemen strippers, now I'm lucky if I take half a dozen. Nowadays all the women want to see is a stripper with a briefcase and bowler hat, peeling off his pinstripe suit to reveal a sensible vest and Y-fronts. It drives them wild."

Meanwhile, ITV have axed the long-running fire drama **London's Burning** and announced plans for a new series set in the world of financial advice. **McGill** will star Robson Green as Keith McGill, a no-nonsense investment analyst in a busy Newcastle accountancy practice, who sometimes has to bend the rules to get results. It will be shown in the autumn, and is expected to go head to head with **Silent Partners,** the BBC drama starring Ross Kemp as Mike Brown, a mortgage arranger in a busy Manchester office who sometimes has to bend the rules to get results.

LOVE ME T

Firemen first topped the hunkiness charts way back in 1911, and they have maintained their position ever since. This year's chart marks the first time in nearly a century that they have been knocked from their number one spot.

Over the years, many professions have challenged them. They came closest to being toppled in 1969, the year of the first Moon landings, when 42% of women would have bedded anything in a spacesuit. But firemen still held on by the narrowest of margins, with 44% of Britain's ladies still longing for a 999 hero between the sheets.

HOT STUFF - Some firemen not yesterday, and how the chart looked in 1911, or something.

AA608

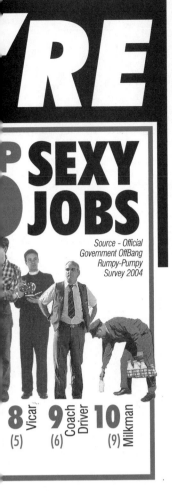
Halifax adverts or hunky money corespondent Declan Curry off BBC Breakfast News. Woof! I've got a wide-on just thinking about them," she added.

To see who has the sexiest job, we asked a fireman and a financial adviser to keep diaries of a typical day at work.

On the Job

CASE 1

Name: Jed Parslow
Age: 24
Occupation: Firefighter, Red Watch, Paddington Green Fire Station, London

8.00am Breakfast is interrupted by a call out to a small electrical fire above a grocer's shop in the High Street. Faulty wiring has ignited some oil-soaked lino behind a cooker. We put the blaze out using a carbon dioxide extinguisher and advise the tenant to invest in a battery-operated smoke alarm and a wall-mounted fire blanket.

10.00am A game of pool in the canteen is interrupted by a call out to rescue a cat which has become stranded up a tree. Since this is not an emergency, we make our way to the incident without lights or sirens operating, and obeying all speed restrictions and traffic signals. When we arrive, the cat has already made its way down the tree and the owner is waiting to apologise for calling us out.

11.00am A group of local Boy Scouts arrive for a pre-arranged look around the station facilities. They are keen to sit in the engine and slide down the pole. They are disappointed when I inform them that, due to Health and Safety regulations, this is not permitted. A photographer from the local paper arrives to take their picture wearing our helmets and oversized jackets.

12.00am We make a routine visit to a local office block to check extinguishers, fire exit signs etc. We find access to an emergency door in one of the offices partially blocked by two boxes of envelopes and refuse to issue a fire safety certificate until the situation has been rectified. People don't realise that in an emergency, moving obstructions from in front of emergency exits can take valuable time. It may only be a second or two, but a second or two in a major fire could mean the difference between life and death. Next we test the smoke alarm batteries in the communal area of the building, and find them all to be in order. Nevertheless, we remind the caretaker of the importance of testing the batteries at least once a week.

12.30pm A game of table tennis at the station is interrupted by a call out to an allotment fire that is threatening to get out of control. Hydrant access is blocked by a parked car, so we use the retardant foam in the tender to extinguish the blaze. It's a small blaze and only two officers are required to deal with this incident, so I remain in the cab, reading the paper and listening to Steve Wright in the Afternoon.

1.15pm On the way back to the station, we call in at the office we visited earlier to check that the boxes of envelopes have been removed. Fortunately they have, so we are able to issue a new fire safety certificate valid for the next twelve months. On our way out, we notice a plug socket in the foyer which has been dangerously overloaded. We always recommend the use of proper BSS standard electrical plugboards with fuses of the appropriate rating, preferably with safety cutout switches to prevent overheating.

2.30pm The Lady Mayoress arrives to ceremonially present us with 3 new sets of breathing apparatus, bought with money raised by the local Rotary Club. She is keen to sit in the engine and slide down the pole but once again Health and Safety regulations mean this is not possible.

4.00pm We are called out to a blaze at a local block of flats where a chip pan has been left unattended and has burst into flames. However, by the time we arrive, a neighbour has extinguished the fire by turning down the heat and covering the pan with a damp tea towel.

5.30pm Shift ends.

CASE 2

Name: Ken O'Dougal
Age: 46
Occupation: Independent Financial Adviser, Portland Associates, Grimsby

8.30am I'm up bright and early for a home visit to a couple who want to finance a loft conversion. When I arrive I'm told by the wife, an attractive, busty blonde in her mid-thirties, that her husband has been unexpectedly called away on business. I take her through the various options, explaining the most tax-efficient ways to extend her endowment mortgage, but she soon makes it clear that she's got another sort of endowment she wants to extend! Before I know it, she's pulled my clothes off and we're having wild, uninhibited sex right there on the kitchen table. After the most explosive orgasm of my life, she fills in the standing order forms while I put my clothes back on.

10.30am I'm back to the office, and there's a lot of paperwork to catch up on. A woman calls in for some financial advice. She has a TESSA that's just matured, and wants some ideas about the best way to invest her tax-free lump sum. However, it soon becomes clear that the tax-free sum isn't the only lump she's interested in! Complaining that my office is hot, she starts to unbutton her dress. Before you can say Financial Services Regulatory Authority we're both stark naked and having wild, doggy-style sex across the photocopier. Suddenly the door opens and my prim secretary walks in with a P111D to sign. When she sees what's going on she takes off her glasses, lets down her hair and joins us for a sexy threesome. After the most intense orgasm of my life, I sign the form and phone my brokers to arrange for my client's profits to be re-invested in a gilt-edged with-profits tracker as she re-arranges her clothing and prepares to leave.

2.00pm An Inland Revenue Inspector arrives, along with her lesbian lover, to discuss an irregularity in one of my clients' tax returns. I turn round to the filing cabinet, looking for the relevant documents but when I look up the two of them have stripped down to their silky lingerie and are putting on one hell of a show. They invite me to join in...but tell me to keep my bowler hat on. I don't need asking twice! After a series of earth-shattering orgasms, it turns out that, because it is a leap year, my client has inadvertently counted February 29th as week 53, when, because she is paid monthly, it should be counted as week 54 and carried over into the next tax year. I can't help wondering if the tax inspector knew that all along.

4.00pm I'm at a local hotel, to chair a seminar of local business leaders discussing the consequences of the Chancellor's pre-budget announcement. Throughout the meeting, I am distracted by an attractive woman who runs a mobile hairdressing salon and keeps crossing and uncrossing her legs. I can see she is wearing no knickers, like Sharon Stone in Basic Instinct. When the seminar is over, I get in the lift to go to the ground floor but just as the doors are closing, she jumps in with me. She asks me if I am "going down" and winks seductively. I press the stop button between floors as she begins to pull my clothes off. Soon she is orally pleasuring me to peaks of pleasure that I can only imagine. My moans of ecstasy set off the fire alarm and we find ourselves drenched by the sprinklers.

5.30pm Home to the wife, who takes my bowler hat and umbrella, and asks me if I've had a nice day at the office. Little does she know!

Dead Poet's Twocker Shocker

By our Poetry and PS2 correspondent **Gladstone Screwer**

Too violent? ~ Betjeman speeds through Slough in a stolen Frazer-Nash shooting brake in the sick video game.

ANGRY campaigners are threatening legal action against high street retailers if they refuse to withdraw the latest violent video game to hit the shelves – chart-topping Playstation smash Grand Theft Laureate.

In the game, set in the late 1950s, players take control of vengeful poet Laureate the late Sir John Betjeman, stealing Humber Alpine motor-cars and slaughtering innocent bystanders with stout sticks in a shocking mixture of bloody mayhem and whimsical poetry about changing trends in post-war British architecture.

Since its release last week, the rhythmic, carnage-heavy Playstation 2 hit has become an obsession for children as young as five, despite its 18-certificate rating.

murder

The object of the game is for the Betjeman character to murder his way around the Home Counties, looking for someone who will draw him a quiet pint of bitter beer, and settle it in an eddying lake of foam on the oak trestle-table of an ivy-wrapped inn. Betjeman must then murder them too.

Dead Poet ~ Betjeman, yesterday.

Josiah Crackerbarrel, head of killjoy pressure group aSaferUK, told reporters who weren't really listening to him: "This game is completely

Betjeman Computer Game Sparks Fears of Poetic Rhyme Wave

disgusting and morally repugnant on every conceivable level."

colonel mustard

"I haven't managed to complete level 7 of Grand Theft Laureate so far," he admitted, "but the subject matter is totally inappropriate. If I'm not having to suffocate a prostitute with a leftover cream bun then I'm being forced to fly a helicopter into the belfry of a picturesque English village church.

"Kids who are exposed to this level of sustained debauchery and elegiac pining for the lost soul of England will unquestionably be scarred for life."

The company responsible for making the game was unavailable for comment as their senior management were too busy pissing themselves over the acres of free publicity they had received as a result of the pompous protests.

captain sensible

Despite the manufacturers' flippancy, the game's critics insist damage is still being done. Last week, a 12-year-old child was detained at a school in Blackburn following the attempted stabbing of one of his classmates. Witnesses say that the boy, James Widdle, who cannot be named for legal reasons, was speaking in four-line stanzas at the time, and wildly trying to rhyme "balustrade" with "orange Lucozade".

UP THE ARSE

Sender ~ Cecil Gaybody, Fulchester

CORNER

...SO THERE I WAS, MANOEUVRING A TROLLEY IN THE ASDA CAR PARK WHEN I GASHED MY THUMB ON A JAGGED PIECE OF METAL...

SO...HA!...OFF I WENT TO THE LOCAL ACCIDENT AND EMERGENCY DEPARTMENT...WELL! YOU CAN IMAGINE THE STIR I CAUSED. A THESPIAN OF MY STANDING ARRIVING IN THEIR HUMBLE LITTLE ESTABLISHMENT!

...BUT I INSISTED—NO STAR TREATMENT! I TOLD THE NURSE, I MAY HAVE TROD THE BOARDS WITH SOME OF THE FINEST TRAGEDIANS OF OUR AGE - OLIVIER, RICHARDSON...CHUCKLE, BOTH PAUL AND BARRY - BUT YOU MUST TREAT ME AS YOU WOULD THE MOST LOWLY CIVILIAN.

AND DO YOU KNOW...THEY DID! BLESS THEIR DARLING HEARTS. ...THEY SPELLED MY NAME WRONG AND LEFT ME WAITING ON A TROLLEY FOR 6 HOURS.

HA! PRICELESS!

...WELL - WHEN I WAS SEEN, THE NURSE - PRETTY YOUNG THING - HAD TO GIVE ME AN INJECTION...

...IN THE DERRIERE! HA!

JUST IMAGINE!

THE POOR GIRL! OF COURSE, SHE PRETENDED NOT TO RECOGNISE ME TO COVER HER EMBARRASSMENT...HA! HA! HAAAAA! HA! HA! HA! HAAAAAAAA!

BUT I COULD SEE SHE KNEW EXACTLY WHO I WAS...NONE OTHER THAN THE ACTOR WHO PLAYED FOURTH STALL-HOLDER FROM THE LEFT IN ALBION MARKET, EPISODE 18....MOI!

WELL I'M SURE SHE'S DINED OUT ON THAT STORY MANY MANY TIMES SINCE - THE TIME SHE SAW LUVVIE DARLING'S BOTTOM-AND I'M NOT...HA! HA! HAAA!...TALKING ABOUT MY LEGENDARY 1981 MIDSUMMER NIGHT'S DREAM OPPOSITE DEAR DEAR STU FRANCIS AND LORRAINE CHASE AT THE...

LUVVIE...DRAYLING?

DRAYLING?...NO NO... DARLING. LUVVIE DARLING...D-A-R-....

NO. IT DEFINITELY SAYS DRAYLING HERE.

COME COME! SURELY YOU HAVE SEEN THIS FACE BEFORE. IT IS I!

ERM...HANG ON. YES.

HOW SILLY OF ME! IT IS YOU, ISN'T IT.

YOU COLLECT THE TROLLEYS IN THE CAR PARK AT ASDA, DON'T YOU.

ANYWAY, MR. DRAYLING, WE'RE SEEING EXTRAS AND SPEAR-CARRIERS ON THURSDAY, SO IF YOU'D LIKE TO POP BACK THEN... WE WERE AUDITIONING FOR THE PART OF ROMEO TODAY.

IT'S DARLING...D-A-R-L-I-N-G! AND IT IS FOR THE RÔLE OF ROMEO FOR WHICH I AM HERE TO ESSAY FOR HERE TODAY, DEAR BOY.

OH, OKAY BUT...

NOW STAND ASIDE, LADDIE. THE STAGE AWAITS MY PRESENCE AND WILL BROOK NO DELAY - FOR THE MUSE OF THESPOS IS UPON ME.

NEXT.

A-HEM

SOFT - WHAT LIGHT FROM YONDER...

ER...STOP YOU THERE...

YES, YES, I KNOW. THAT WAS MY 'METHOD' APPROACH. I SEE YOU'D PREFER SOMETHING SLIGHTLY MORE FROM THE STANISLAVSKY SCHOOL...

A-HEM

SOFT - WHAT LIGHT FROM YONDER...

...STOP YOU THERE AGAIN, MR. DRAYLING. IT'S EXTRAS AND SPEAR-CARRIERS ON THURSDAY.

WE'RE CALLING ROMEOS TODAY.

ROMEO, DEAR HEART, IS THE VERY PART IN WHICH I AM INTERESTED... ...IN.

OH, I SEE. WELL... IT WAS VERY GOOD, MR. DRAYLING... I LIKED WHAT YOU DID... LOVED IT. NEVER SEEN BETTER...

...BUT YOU'RE NOT QUITE WHAT WE'RE LOOKING FOR IN THIS PRODUCTION...

DING DONG

...cough...

OH. THAT WILL BE THE PRIEST NOW.

HE'S COME NOT A MOMENT TOO SOON.

CEDRIC IS FADING FAST AND HAS LITTLE ENOUGH TIME TO RECEIVE HIS LAST RITES.

FATHER O'BRIEN, THANK THE LORD YOU'VE ARRIVED IN TIME.

SORRY I'M LATE, THERE WAS A TRIPLE BILL OF AMERICA'S DUMBEST CRIMINALS ON BRAVO.

MY HUSBAND IS UPSTAIRS, FATHER. THE DOCTOR SAYS HE COULD GO ANY MOMENT.

OOH, DO YOU MIND IF I POP THAT TELLY ON? PETROCELLI IS ABOUT TO START ON GRANADA PLUS.

AH, NOW YOU SEE THAT BLOKE STANDING BEHIND PETROCELLI, HE WAS IN KNIGHT RIDER.

HE PLAYED MICHAEL LANDON'S BOSS IN THE FIRST COUPLE OF SERIES.

NOT MICHAEL LANDON, I MEAN DAVID HASSELHOFF. MICHAL LANDON WAS HIM OUT OF LITTLE HOUSE ON THE PRAIRIE.

KNIGHT RIDER WAS DAVID HASSELHOFF.

WILL YOU COME UP AND SEE TO MY CEDRIC NOW, FATHER?

YOU REMEMBER KNIGHT RIDER'S TALKING CAR, WELL THE BLOKE WHO DID THE VOICE OF THE CAR WAS THAT ONE OUT OF QUANTUM LEAP WITH THE CIGAR.

WHAT'S HIS NAME, I KEEP THINKING OF HARRY DEAN STANTON, BUT IT'S NOT HIM. HE WAS IN BLUE VELVET.

NO HANG ON IT'S NOT HIM AT ALL, IT'S THAT OTHER GUY, WHO WAS IN ST ELSEWHERE

CEDRIC, LOVE? FATHER O'BRIEN IS HERE.

WILLIAM SOMETHING. BEGINS WITH A 'D'.

FATHER... I'M READY TO MAKE MY FINAL CONFESSION...

CLICK

OH! YOU'VE GOT A PORTABLE UP HERE. WE'LL JUST HAVE IT ON IN THE BACKGROUND SHALL WE?

.. I'VE ALWAYS TRIED TO LEAD A RIGHTEOUS LIFE, FATHER... BUT THERE HAVE BEEN TIMES WHEN I...

ARE YOU LISTENING TO ME, FATHER?

SORRY, I WAS JUST THINKING, WASN'T THAT WOMAN IN THE BLUE DRESS WOLFIE SMITH'S GIRLFRIEND'S MUM IN CITIZEN SMITH?

NO, WAIT, I'M THINKING OF HER IN THAT EPISODE OF FAWLTY TOWERS WHO GETS GIVEN THE RAW MACKEREL.

NOW THAT BLOKE NEXT TO HER, THE ONE OUT OF SHINE ON HARVEY MOON, HE ALWAYS TURNS UP IN POIROT. CHRIST, WHAT'S HIS NAME AGAIN?

HE WAS IN THAT SERIES WHERE MARMALADE ATKINS PLAYED A LESBIAN. I ALWAYS GET HIM MIXED UP WITH PETE POSTLETHWAITE.

IS..IS IT ALUN ARMSTRONG, FATHER?

NO, NO, NO, ALUN ARMSTRONG'S GOT THE BUSHY EYEBROWS, CRAGGY FACE, USED TO CROP UP IN THE SWEENEY.

EVERYTHING'S GOING BLACK, FATHER... I'M FLOATING DOWN A LONG TUNNEL...

OH GOD, WHAT IS THIS BLOKE'S NAME? THIS IS REALLY GOING TO BUG ME. TIMOTHY SOMETHING. TIMOTHY.... TIMOTHY... NOT TIMOTHY SPALL...

KENNETH CRANHAM, THAT'S HIM!

CROAK!

THUMP

MY HUSBAND — HE'S GONE! AND HE NEVER GOT THE CHANCE TO MAKE HIS PEACE WITH GOD.

HE WAS IN BERGERAC, AS WELL.

I'M VERY UPSET ABOUT THIS, FATHER. CEDRIC WAS ENTITLED TO RECEIVE HIS LAST RITES, AND ALL YOU GAVE HIM WAS A BARRAGE OF TELEVISION TRIVIA.

HMM?

I SHALL BE COMPLAINING TO THE BISHOP ABOUT THIS.

AND SO— FATHER O'BRIEN IS DEEPLY SORRY FOR THE DISTRESS HE CAUSED YOU, MRS POBJOY.

BISHOP

HE HAS BEEN SUFFERING FROM EMOTIONAL PROBLEMS RECENTLY, BUT HE ASSURES ME HE IS MUCH BETTER NOW.

HOWEVER, TO SET YOU MIND AT EASE, I WILL PERSONALLY BE OVERSEEING YOUR LATE HUSBAND'S FUNERAL SERVICE.

THANK YOU, BISHOP.

AND— ..NO, NO, JOANNA LUMLEY WAS IN THE **NEW** AVENGERS, THE ORIGINAL AVENGERS HAD DIANA RIGG, HONOR BLACKMAN...

WELL THAT'S DEFINITELY KATE O'MARA, NOW SHE TURNED UP IN TRIANGLE...

ROGER MELLIE
THE MAN ON THE TELLY

WELL, THAT'S ALL FOR THIS MORNING'S DISCUSSION 'MEN'S COCKS: IS BIGGER BETTER?' JOIN US TOMORROW ON 'ROGER' WHEN OUR TOPIC WILL BE..

'...WOMEN'S TITS... IS BIGGER BETTER?'

WELL THAT WENT VERY WELL I THOUGHT, TOM. ALWAYS NICE TO END WITH A BIT OF A RUCK

ROGER...

GOOD FOR THE RATINGS

COME ON, TOM. FANCY A TRIP TO THE BEEB BAR FOR A SPOT OF BREAKFAST?

ROGER...

MORNING MR. MELLIE. THE USUAL, IS IT?

MAKE IT A TREBLE, GREG... WORKED UP A BIT OF AN APPETITE TODAY

SO WHO'S LINED UP FOR THE TIT DEBATE TOMORROW THEN, TOM?

ROGER...

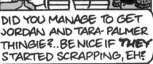

DID YOU MANAGE TO GET JORDAN AND TARA-PALMER THINGIE?... BE NICE IF **THEY** STARTED SCRAPPING, EH?

ROGER... I'VE BEEN TRYING TO TELL YOU. THERE ISN'T GOING TO BE A SHOW TOMORROW

FUCKIN' HELL! IS IT FRIDAY ALREADY, TOM? GET IN!

NO. THE SHOW HAS BEEN **AXED**... BECAUSE OF THIS COLUMN YOU WROTE

EH?

... "MY KIND OF DAY"

WHAT?.. THERE ISN'T ANYTHING CONTROVERSIAL IN THIS...

...TAKING THE DOG FOR A WALK... WHAT I HAD FOR DINNER... THE USUAL BOLLOCKS

IT'S SOFT AS SHITE, TOM. CAN'T SEE WHAT THEY'RE OBJECTING TO

HMM!..

IT'S NOT **WHAT** YOU SAID, ROGER, SO MUCH AS WHERE YOU CHOSE TO SAY IT.

THEIR MONEY'S AS GOOD AS ANYONE'S, TOM. JUST BECAUSE I WRITE A COLUMN FOR THEM EVERY WEEK DOESN'T MEAN I SHARE ALL THEIR BELIEFS.

LEBENS REALM
BRITAIN'S BEST SELLING NAZI WEEKLY
THE TRUTH ABOUT THE HOLOCAUST
Plus TV'S ROGER MELLIE "my kind of day"

ANYWAY, THE FACT REMAINS THAT YOUR DAYTIME SHOW HAS BEEN DROPPED FROM THE SCHEDULES

AH! STORM IN A TEACUP

Sun NAZI MELLIE DROPPED

WHAT? THE PRESS ARE AFTER YOUR **BLOOD**, ROGER... AND **DON'T** SAY 'TOMORROW'S FI...'

TOMORROW'S FISH AND CHIP PAPER

RACE HATE ROGER AND OUT SHOW AXED

C'MON... LET'S HAVE A SIT DOWN

ANYWAY... FUCK THAT, TOM. IF YOU CHECK THE TELLY PAGE, YOU'LL SEE I'M ON **ROOM 101** TONIGHT... BOOKED BEFORE ALL THIS SHIT BLEW UP

EH!?.. OH, SO YOU ARE

SO EVERYTHING WILL BE FINE, THEN

EH!? HOW DO YOU MEAN?

YOU WAIT AND SEE... I'LL DO A FEW GAGS ABOUT MY CHOICES... TRAFFIC WARDENS, CONES ON MOTORWAYS, MILK CARTONS, THAT SORT OF THING...

SHOW THEM I'M A MAN OF THE PEOPLE, TOM. SOON GET THE PUBLIC BACK ON MY SIDE.

HMM... WELL... I SUPPOSE IT MIGHT...

MOBILE PHONES ON TRAINS, THERE'S ANOTHER, TOM.

HA! YES, ROGER. ON TRAINS... HA! **TOO RIGHT!**

YOU KNOW, THIS MAY JUST WORK

YEAH! IT'S GOING OUT LIVE TONIGHT.

TOMORROW MORNING THEY'LL BE BEGGING ME TO COME BACK... AND IT WON'T BE SOME TINPOT DAYTIME SHIT, NEITHER... NO!..

IT'LL BE THE SATURDAY NIGHT 7 O'CLOCK SLOT... AND I'LL NAME MY PRICE.

THAT NIGHT...

LADIES AND GENTLEMEN, WELCOME TO ROOM 101. MY GUEST TONIGHT IS THE CONTROVERSIAL BROADCASTER

ROGER MELLIE!

ROOM 101

NOW, ROGER. YOU'VE MADE SOME INTERESTING CHOICES OF THINGS TO BE BANISHED INTO ROOM 101... TRAFFIC WARDENS, O.A.P. DRIVERS, MOBILE PHONES ON TRAINS. BUT WHAT'S YOUR FIRST CHOICE?

MY FIRST CHOICE, PAUL, IS...

...THE BLACKS!

101

NEXT DAY...

WELL, I THINK I WENT A BIT TOO FAR THIS TIME... I THINK MY CAREER MIGHT BE OVER, TOM.

NO!..

Sun MELLIE ARRESTED ON AIR

THAT WAS THE BBC ON THE PHONE. THEY WANT TO KNOW IF YOU FANCY STANDING IN FOR JIM DAVIDSON ON THE GENERATION GAME NEXT WEEK

Letterbocks

Letterbocks Letterbocks Letterbocks

Letterbocks, Viz Comic, PO Box 1PT, Newcastle upon Tyne NE99 1PT

★ The saying goes, 'See a penny, pick it up, and all day long you'll have good luck.' Well I beg to differ. I'm a matador, and whilst picking a penny up at work the other day I was badly gored in the anus. That's not good luck in my book.

Milos el Standish
Barcelona

★ I've just finished watching *Crimewatch UK*, and at the end, Nick Ross said 'Do sleep well and don't have nightmares'. How does he expect me to sleep well when he's just shown the nation a video of me doing an armed robbery on a post office in Worksop?

Dave Gell
Mansfield

★ I was infuriated to read in my local copy of Metro this week that '10,000 terrorists were ready to strike at any moment.' It's bad enough that they are responsible for death and destruction, but to think they are now going to push for better working conditions really maes my blood boil.

Matthew Sparks
e-mail

In this space age you can electromail your letters and tips to **letters@viz.co.uk**

★ I have just finished watching the D-Day 60th anniversary celebrations on television, and I have to say that I am surprised we won, seeing as so many of our soldiers seem to be in wheelchairs. It must have been a real struggle just getting up the beach, let alone having to dodge bullets.

Duncan Horastead
e-mail

★ It doesn't seem a problem that Home Secretary David Blunkett is hell bent on introducing ID cards when the country is against it - we could just tell him that we've got them already. If he asks to check somebody's card, they could just hand him a credit card or a Blockbusters video card or something.

Ollie Tate
Leeds

★ The other week I was caught speeding by a Gatso camera and issued with a £60 fine and 3 points on my licence through the post. However, had there been a police patrol there, they would have noticed that I was at least twice the legal drink drive limit, with four bald tyres and an out of date tax disc. People often complain that these cameras are a moneyspinner for the government, but this one actually saved me a lot of money and a certain ban. Well done Gatso.

Richard Karslake
Oxfordshire

So called 'ladette' Sara Cox claims she can 'drink like the men.'Well, she should have come out with me 2 years ago. I would have to knock back half a bottle of vodka to get out of the house. Then I'd spend the rest of the day roaming the streets of Bromley, mumbling to myself, shouting at pensioners and drinking endless litres of strong cider. This would continue untill I soiled myself and slept where I fell. After a 6-month re-hab, I now attend regular 12-step meetings and stay sober, 'a day at a time.' Face it, Coxy, you're not in my league.

Kent Pete
Kent

★ Captain Scott may have been only the second man to reach the South Pole, but he was the first to die there. So his expedition wasn't a total waste of time.

TC Rusling
Cottingham

★ It's disgusting. When Saddam Hussain was caught, the first thing that happened was he recieved a full dental check-up. I have been waiting over 2 years to see an NHS dentist in my home town of Bromley. Perhaps I should attempt mass genocide, then I might get seen a bit quicker.

Kent Pete
Kent

★ In response to last Letterbocks page's Star Letter (Fox's biscuits, Chinese chefs, bum rape), I would point the writer and his unfortunate friend towards the Fox's Party Ring as our recommended biscuit for this occasion.

Ed Miles
Foxes Biscuits

STAR LETTER

HOW happy Andy Williams sounds as he trills out the line 'The boys watch the girls while the girls watch the boys who watch the girls go by'. Why can't social services adopt a similar carefree attitude when moving me on from the local primary school?

J. Richardson, Merseyside

Vent Your Spleen

This week's Hot Topic:
Des O'Connor
~ proud dad or dirty dog?

O'Connor ~ spilling his spendings

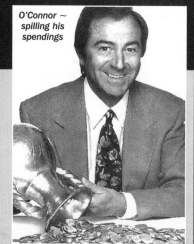

THE NEWS that entertainer Des O'Connor is to be a father again at the age of 72 has been met by mixed reactions in the press. Some commentators have congratulated the evergreen veteran singer on his virility, whilst others have condemned his sordid behaviour. We went out on the streets to gauge the public's mood.

"...I think that what Des has done is disgusting beyond words. I own a pram shop and if that dirty old orange man came in to buy one, I'd sell him faulty goods and charge him double. I might even short change him."
Sid Pamplemouse, Shopkeeper

"...O'Connor ought to be thoroughly ashamed of himself. Every time I think of his wizened old penis penetrating his wife's fresh, unsullied vagina, thrusting in and out, in and out towards orgasm, before finally spurting his septuagenarian spendings through the neck of her innocent young womb, I get sick to my stomach."
Mrs Thrush, Housewife

"...Anyone fathering a child at such an advanced age is a blasphemy against nature. Rather than patting him on the back as some newspapers seem to be doing, they should be calling for him to be chemically castrated."
Edna Carstairs, Busybody

"...I hope Des can afford some nappies after spending all that money on Viagra!"
Roy Hudd, Veteran Comedian

"...When I heard the news on the BBC that 72-year-old Des O'Connor had got his wife pregnant, I was so appalled that I put my foot through the telly...and sent him the bill."
Mr Collis, Retired Welder

"...The baby will have to sleep in Des and his wife's bed for the first few weeks. The nursery is full of empty Viagra boxes!"
Roy Hudd, Shit Comic

"...I think it's lovely that Des is to become a dad again so late in life. The child will look on its father as a mature and stable influence - something the children of younger fathers often sadly lack. Also, when they play football with him in the park the old fart will be piss easy to beat."
Anton de Putain, Retired Murderer

"...When I read the news in the paper, I was so appalled I put my foot through the page... and sent him the bill."
Mr Collis, Retired Welder

"Des's first baby, Mary, was conceived on the Queen Mary, and his second child, Snowdon, was conceived on Mount Snowdon. I hear this baby's going to be called Viagra!"
Roy Hudd, Unentertainer

"...Has Des O'Connor stopped for a moment to think that when this child is a teenager, he will be in his mid-eighties and unable to discuss soap operas, pop bands and computer games? What's more, when the child is as old as Des is now, Des will be nearly a hundred and fifty years old, and unable to discuss rocket packs, hover cars and teleportation devices."
Tarquin Ballache, Soothsayer

"...My wife told me the news. I was so incensed that I put my foot through my wife, and sent Des O'Connor the bill."
Mr Collis, Retired Welder

"...Erm...What's long, hard and full of semen? Des O'Connor's submarine...on Viagra!"
Roy Hudd, Not Funnyman

★ They say 'No News is Good News'. That's a great comfort to me. My uncle recently went out to Iraq as a Christian Missionary to promote the word of the true God. As I have heard no word from him in the past six months, I can only assume that things are going swimmingly.

William Harrington
e-mail

★ Nesquik Milkshake claims to be "So Fun to Make!" on the packet. Imagine my disappointment when on making some, I found that it was no better than average.

Mark Entwistle
Bucks

★ I'm fed up with finding my e-mail inbox stuffed full of adverts for penis enlarging pills. In the interests of sexual equality, isn't it about time that they started bombarding women's computers with adverts for fanny tightening tablets?

Neil
Scotland

★ I went to the cinema the other day, but it was rubbish. Come on, film makers, make some decent films.

M Baker
Barnstaple

TOP TIPS

HOMEOWNERS. Don't hesitate to tell the rest of us how much your house has appreciated in value since you bought it. The more frequently you give us updates, the greater will be our delight at your good fortune and our admiration and respect for your financial prescience.

Paul Bradshaw
e-mail

DEAF people. Wearing oven gloves outdoors is an ideal way to stop strangers from eavesdropping on your conversation.

Ian Knott
Working

NATURALISTS. Make your own otter by doing bonsai on a seal.

Julian Barlow
Coggeshall

GENTLEMEN. Speed up your lovemaking by playing Benny Hill's theme tune *'Yackety Sax'* in the bedroom.

Fisk Kid
e-mail

GRATED cheddar cheese from the supermarket can be squashed tightly together with the fingers to produce a block of cheese, ready for slicing or grating.

Reginald
e-mail

BLIND people. Give yourself at least a chance of seeing something by not wearing heavy dark glasses all the time.

James Smyth
Hitchin

EACH month, put a pet mouse down the back of your sofa for a few hours. Hey Presto, all loose biscuit crumbs will be eaten.

Jason Richardson
Wallasey

FOOTBALL teams. Fed up with good attacking play being let down by the final ball? Simply plan your moves to end one pass quicker and watch the goals fly in.

Steve Fitzpatrick
Birmingham

It's YOUR chance to...
Spew your Bile

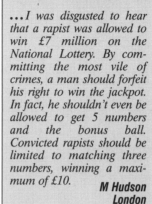

CONVICTED rapist **Iorworth Hoare**'s £7million win on the national lottery has sparked a storm of protest across the land. Never in the history of Letterbocks have Viz readers' danders been so gotten up. Here are a selection of the letters we received...

* *

...*I was disgusted to hear that a rapist was allowed to win £7 million on the National Lottery. By committing the most vile of crimes, a man should forfeit his right to win the jackpot. In fact, he shouldn't even be allowed to get 5 numbers and the bonus ball. Convicted rapists should be limited to matching three numbers, winning a maximum of £10.*

M Hudson
London

...To prevent further rapists winning £7 million on the lottery whilst law abiding citizens miss out, the current system of numbers and balls should be scrapped. Everyone should pay £1 as they do now, and the person who has committed the least number of sexual offences should win the jackpot. They then do not enter the lottery again. This way, everybody will eventually win a jackpot, and rapists will have to wait a long time and win a significantly smaller sum.

L French
Peterborough

...*I spend over £30 a week on lottery tickets and scratch cards and the most I have ever won is £10. perhaps if I went out and raped somebody, the powers that be at the National Lottery would come round and give me 7 million quid. Come on, Camelot, get your act together.*

M Winterborough
Carlisle

...A rapist winning £7 million on the National Lottery? What is the world coming to? My son is no rapist, only ever having been convicted of a series of aggravated sexual assaults, and the most he has won is 58 grand when he got 5 numbers and the bonus ball. It doesn't seen fair.

T Plywood
Yorkshire

What I don't understand is, if God can part the Red Sea and make it rain biscuits on the Jews or whatever, why can't He jiggle a few ping-pong balls a bit in order to prevent a rapist winning the lottery? I can't see why He doesn't fix it for deserving people, like Mother Teresa, or Terry Waite to scoop the jackpot every week. It has certainly shaken my faith in Him.

Rev. J Foucault
Truro

soap dish

with Jo Soap

LOUD-MOUTHED Oasis funnyman Liam Gallagher is to join the cast of Coronation Street, ITV has announced.

Four-letter-word Liam, 30, will play Deirdre Barlow's long-lost son, Keith Berk, an unemployed millionaire.

Bosses at the daft northern soap are said to have a big entry planned for the character of Berk, who will arrive behind the bar of the Rover's Return in a helicopter.

Plots are being kept under 24-hour lock and key, although insiders say that Liam's flashy character will buy the street and turn it into a theme park called Working Class World.

A source close to Liam told reporters, "He's a fucking cunt like that, our kid."

SPOT THE GEORDIE

© B.TIN 2002

SPAWNY GET

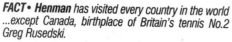

Here it is! Your FREE cut out and keep

TIM HENMAN
FACT FILE

TIM FACT FILE

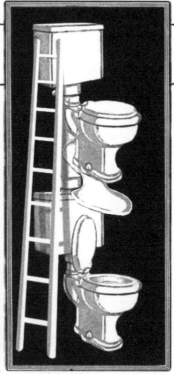

FACT• **Henman** has visited every country in the world ...except Canada, birthplace of Britain's tennis No.2 Greg Rusedski.

FACT• **Tim** was born in 1974.

FACT• **Tim** is 32 years old.

FACT• **Tim's** fave pop group is Busted.

FACT• In 1994, Tim celebrated his 20th birthday.

FACT• In a year, Tim will reach the grand old age of 33!

FACT• The lead singer of Tim's favourite group, Busted, is called Charlie.

FACT• When Charlie, the lead singer of Tim's favourite group, Busted, was born, Tim was 12 years old.

FACT• When Charlie, the lead singer of Tim's favourite group, Busted, is as old as Tim is now, Tim will be 44.

FACT• When not playing tennis, Tim likes to relax at night by putting on pyjamas, lying on a bed, and shutting his eyes for up to 8 hours.

FACT• **Tim** shares his favourite vegetable with former mediocre F1 star Damon Hill.

FACT• **Tim** is looking forward to receiving a telegram from the Queen in 2074, when he'll celebrate his 100th birthday.

FACT• **Charlie**, lead singer of Busted, Tim's favourite band, doesn't share his favourite vegetable with either Tim or former mediocre F1 star Damon Hill. He shares it with excitable Sky TV soccer pundit Andy Gray.

FACT• Most people have a cat or a dog as a pet, but not Tim! His pet is most unusual.

Dial M1 for MURDER

Plans to install hundreds of new murder cameras by the sides of British roads have been greeted with furious protests from the country's lorry drivers.

Under the new scheme, anyone caught on camera committing a roadside murder will be automatically sent a photograph of the incident, together with a summons and a fine. The cameras are intended to speed up processing times for layby homicide, but anti-camera lobbyists insist they are just a way to increase police revenue and persecute law abiding murderers.

BLACKSPOTS

Freight Handler's Union boss Bob Small spoke for many of his members yesterday. "We don't mind the police

putting these things up at notorious murder blackspots, like where the patio used to be behind Fred West's house, but the new sites seem to have been chosen deliberately to catch innocent lorry drivers as they go about their daily business of rolling dead backpackers up in carpet and throwing them onto the hard shoulder."

"It's just giving the police an HGV licence to print money. The truckers may be doing the murders, but it's the police that are making the killing," added Mr Small.

BLACKHEADS

Complaints have also been made that the new cameras have been made deliberately hard to spot – concealed behind trees and roadsigns and painted in drab colours.

"The first thing you know is the flash of the blasted thing going off," said Graham Uppity, a lorry driver who clocks up over a dozen hitch-hikers a year. "If they made them a bit more obvious, you could stop murdering when you saw one. The way I see it, it's just another way to line the coppers' pockets so they can buy gold handcuffs and whistles with rubies instead of peas."

IAN DURY

Representatives of Murdering Associations such as the MA and RMC have also complained that murder cameras may not be completely reliable, resulting in lorry drivers being fined for killings for which they were not responsible. The scheme received widespread negative publicity last year after a haulier received an automatic penalty for a murder committed on the M25. However, he was later able to

successfully prove that at the time of the offence he was 360 miles away committing a rape in a layby near Leeds.

IAN BRADY

"I want to know what the police are doing about the real villains," demanded Mr Uppity. "They should be out looking for people like Dr Octopus, Bluto, and Skeletor, rather than persecuting hard working truckers who want nothing more than to get to their destinations and dispose of their victims as quickly as possible".

And TV's motormouth petrolhead motormouth Jeremy Clarkson was quick to side with the truckers. "Lorry drivers travel hundreds of miles every day up and down the motorways delivering all sorts of goods, keeping the wheels of industry turning. They are the life-blood of the British economy. Not content with heavy fuel prices, the government now wants to make their job even harder by slapping fines on them each time they murder. I don't know about you, but I think the odd corpse here and there is a small price to pay for our supermarket shelves being fully stocked."

Police estimate that murder cameras save up to 400 lives a year, as well as reducing the build up of suspiciously lumpy tarpaulins in laybys by up to 30% in areas where they are used.

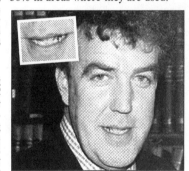

Clarkson's petrol head and *(inset)* his motormouth.

MURDER ON THE ROADS

BRITAIN'S FIVE MOST LUCRATIVE MURDER CAMERAS

A1 NORTH YORKSHIRE Barton Park Services, a favourite stop for truck drivers sees up to 12 murders every week. Locals fear that lorry drivers will take detours through nearby villages slaying residents to avoid the newly installed cameras.

A40 OXFORDSHIRE The layby on the eastbound carriageway near Whitney has long been a favourite for body disposal. A sneaky camera on a nearby bridge has raised over £70,000 since its installation in 2003

M5 SOMERSET Young people hitch hiking to Cornwall make this stretch of road popular with murderous lorry drivers. Five cameras installed by spoilsport Avon and Somerset police have seen the death toll halved.

A470 MONMOUTHSHIRE A quiet road winding through the bleak Brecon Beacons, popular with hikers makes for ideal murdering conditions. But truckers now risk a £200 fine if they strangle someone within view of one of the three murder cameras installed since the new year.

A429 GLOUCESTERSHIRE The heavily wooded area of the Forest of Dean has traditionally been the site of many shallow graves. A mobile camera unit in the area caught 23 truckers burying corpses on its first day of operation.

8 ACE
...ZZ-ZZZ-ZZZ... WIFFLE-WAFFLE ZZ-ZZZ...
...MUMBLE...
ZZZ-LERRUZIN YER F-F-ZZZZ B-BB-BBITCH... ZZ WIFFLE-WAFFLE ZZZ ...WAIN'T BRAY T'B-BBAIRNS... NO MORE ACE... ZZZ-ZZZ...
NEVEH! ZZZ...
ZZZZ-ZZZ-ZZ-ZZ... EIGHT ACE, PLEASE.... ZZZ-ZZ...
WIFFLE-WAFFLE
BLAM! BLAM! BLAM! BLAM!
EH..? WOSSAT!?.. F-FF-FUCK OFF A'M 'AVIN' A NICE NAP AN' A PISS.
BLAM! BLAM! BLAM! BLAM!
AW... F-FF-FFF-FF-FFUCK.
WORRISSIT?
'OW MANY F-FFUCKIN' TIMES DO A 'AVE TER TELL YER, LUV... A NEVEH SPENT THE BBAIRNS'S SUNNEH DEE MUNNY ON ACE.
A SPENT IT ON... SUMMIT ELSE... NOT ACE... SUMMIT GOOD... THAT WAN'T ACE...
ULF!... OO... OO... OO THE F-FFUCK ARE YOO?
I AM THE GRIM REAPER.
AND I HAVE COME TO TAKE YOU, OCTAVIUS TINSWORTH ACE...
WOT THE F-FFUCK FOH? A'VE DUN F-FFUCKIN' NOWT, ME.
EXACTLY, OCTAVIUS TINSWORTH ACE...
YOU HAVE DONE NOTHING DURING YOUR MISERABLE TIME ON THIS EARTH...
NOTHING BUT DRINK CHEAP LAGER AND STRIKE YOUR CHILDREN....
HEY! HEY!.. A F-FFUCKIN' LUV THEM B-BBAIRNS, ME. A'VE NEVEH LAID A F-FF-FF FFUCKIN' FINGEH ON 'EM. IT'S NOT ME WOT BRAYS 'EM.. IT'S THE ACE.
THE F-FFUCKIN' ACE IS USIN' ME AS A CONDUIT FER ITS EVIL WAYS.
BE THAT AS IT MAY, YOU ARE BEING CALLED TO ACCOUNT FOR YOUR ACTIONS, OCTAVIUS TINSWORTH ACE.
BURRIT'S NOT MY F-FFUCKIN' F-FFAULT... IT'S 'ER. A AWNLEH DRINK TH'ACE 'COS SHE DUN'T LERRUZ INT'FFUCKIN' 'OUSE.
SHE'S A F-FFUCKIN' B-BB-BB-BBITCH AN' SO A'VE SOUGHT SOLACE IN'T BOTTOM OF EIGHT TINS. THAT F-FFUCKIN' ACE 'AS BIN ME AWNLEH FRIEND.
SNIFF
BUT NOW IT'S BRANG US TER THIS AN' A CAN SEE IT FER WOT IT IS...
...RIGHT F-FF-FFUCKIN' PISS.
BURRA TELL YER... GIZ ANOTHEH F-FFUCKIN' CHANCE... AN' A'LL CHANGE... A WILL. LERRUZ LIVE AN' NEVEH ANOTHEH DROP O' THE ACE WILL A 'AVE... 'ONEST.
ONE MORE CHANCE... SNIFF ONE MORE CHANCE... THAT'S AALL A FFUCKIN' NEED...
VERY WELL...
EH!?
YOUR PITIFUL PLEADING HAS MOVED ME. I SHALL GRANT YOU ONE CHANCE TO DO A WORTHY ACT IN YOUR WORTHLESS LIFE.
OUTSIDE PATEL'S 24-HOUR NANDMART STANDS A SCOPE CHARITY COLLECTOR. TAKE THIS £1.49 AND PUT IT IN HIS TIN. DO THIS AND YOU WILL BE GIVEN A SECOND CHANCE ON THIS EARTH...
FAIL... AND YOUR LIFE SHALL BE FORFEIT, OCTAVIUS TINS-WORTH ACE. YOU WILL BE CALLED TO ACCOUNT IN THE NEXT WORLD.
THANK-YOU! CHEERS, PAL... A'LL NOT LET YER DAHN... THIS IS IT FER ME... IT'S ME FINAL F-FFUCKIN' CHANCE.
...SPASTICS, NOT ACE... SPASTICS... NOT ACE... NOT ACE... NO. NOT ACE... SPASTICS...
ME LIFE DEPENDS ON IT...
10 MINUTES LATER...
OI! LERRUZ IN THIS F-FF-FFFUCKIN' PARADISE YER ROTTON F-FFUCKIN' B-BB-BASTODS!
FUCK OFF!
IF WE LET YOU IN YOU'LL BRAY THE CHERUBIM.
A F-FFUCKIN' WILL NOT. A LUV THEM CHERUBIM, ME.

JACK BLACK AND THE CHICKEN MYSTERY

THE CHINESE NEW YEAR HOLIDAYS WERE HERE AGAIN, AND BOY SLEUTH JACK BLACK, AND HIS DOG DETECTIVE SILVER, WERE STAYING WITH HIS AUNT MEG IN HER CONVERTED PIT HEAD WINDING HOUSE IN THE TINY WELSH VILLAGE OF LLANGOGOGOGOGOCH.

...NO, MR. BOND... I EXPECT YOU TO DIE!

WHHIIIRRRRRRR!

JACK! WHAT ON EARTH ARE YOU TWO DOING?

WE'RE MAKING A JAMES BOND FILM WITH UNCLE SBONCYN'S CINE CAMERA, AUNT MEG. I'M AURIC GOLDFINGER AND THIS FROG IS JAMES BOND.

WOOF!

OH, AND SILVER IS CUBBY BROCCOLI.

WELL, COME IN, MR. GOLDFINGER. IT'S TIME FOR YOUR LUNCH.

HOORAY! I'M STARVED.

THERE YOU ARE. CHEESE AND PICKLE SANDWICHES.

CHEESE AND PICKLE SANDWICHES? BUT I THOUGHT WE WERE HAVING ROAST CHICKEN FOR LUNCH.

WELL SO DID I, JACK, BUT I COULDN'T GET THE GIBLETS OUT.

HMM! IT LOOKS LIKE MR SHIPTON THE BUTCHER HAS PUSHED THEM UP TOO FAR. THAT'S A SHAME.

WELL I DON'T KNOW WHY HE DOES IT, BUT IT'S THE FIFTH ONE I'VE BOUGHT THIS WEEK LIKE THAT.

THE FIFTH!?!

WELL, I'M GOING TO TAKE IT BACK AND COMPLAIN... COME ON, SILVER.

JACK AND SILVER RACED TO THE BUTCHERS WITH THE CHICKEN, BUT THEY FOUND MR SHIPTON NONE TOO APOLOGETIC...

WHAT DO YOU MEAN, THE GIBLETS ARE TOO FAR UP? EEC HEALTH REGULATIONS STATE THAT GIBLETS MUST BE FAR ENOUGH INSIDE THE CHICKEN SO THAT THEY CANNOT FALL OUT.

OH!

I DON'T WANT TO GET INTO TROUBLE, SO I PUSH THEM UP WITH A BROOM HANDLE...

...PEOPLE WOULD SOON START COMPLAINING IF THE GIBLETS WERE FALLING OUT OVER THE FLOOR AS THEY LEFT THE SHOP. IT WOULD BE SO UNHYGIENIC.

AND SPEAKING OF HYGIENE, GET THAT DOG OUT OF MY SHOP!

RIGHT, SORRY!

BACK HOME, JACK EXPLAINED TO AUNT MEG WHAT HAD HAPPENED...

...SO HE SAID THAT THEY HAD TO BE PUSHED THAT DEEP INTO THE CHICKEN BECAUSE OF EEC REGULATIONS. THOSE BARMY BRUSSELS BUREAUCRATS.

RULES ARE RULES, JACK.

I KNOW, BUT SOMETHING WASN'T RIGHT AND I CAN'T PUT MY FINGER ON IT. HE WAS HIDING SOMETHING.

WELL, I WISH YOU'D HIDE IN YOUR BEDROOM SO I CAN GET THE HOOVERING DONE.

WAIT A MINUTE... THAT'S IT!

SHIPTON SAID HE USED A BROOM HANDLE TO PUSH THE GIBLETS UP THE CHICKENS...

...BUT WHEN WE WERE IN HIS SHOP I SAW HE HAD A VACUUM CLEANER IN THE BACK ROOM.

WOOF!

Cliff's Eye for the Boys

Cliff Richard has stunned friends and fans by sensationally announcing that one of His eyes is *GAY*.

The 63-year-old all-rounder, who had a hit in 1963 and 1997 with Summer Holiday, says the irregularity was discovered by His doctor during a recently expensive consultation.

EXCLUSIVE

"Apparently, this is quite common," Sir Clifford told passing reporters yesterday. "One in a million men suffers. I've spoken to the famous singer Mr David Bowie and he tells me he has a similar problem.

PERCH

Radio Two-friendly Cliff, whose youthful looks have made many a housewife perch on the washing machine during the spin cycle, says He's comfortable with the idea of having an ungodly optic.

"It's perfectly consistent with My beliefs," He continued over a glass of delicious Vida Nova red wine (made at His vineyard at Quinta do Moinha in Portugal, and available at Waitrose for £7.99).

"If God's not unhappy with gay vicars, I'm sure he'll turn a blind eye to My gay eye," quipped the crooning Christian.

BREAM

"I'm looking on the bright side. People have often wondered whether I have an eye for the ladies – and I have – but I've also got one for the gentlemen too!"

Cliff's personal life has always

Queer eye for the straight guy ~ Cliff's heterosexual eye (above, left) and his is-it-or-isn't-it eye (above, right).

been shrouded in discretion, although He has been romantically linked to a famous tennis player and a cartoon rabbit.

So will His gay eye now be 'out' painting the town red?

"Hey, I could get a pair of specially adapted glasses, with one butch lens and one rose-tinted one," he laughed.

MELVYN'S MONSTER TRUCK

MELVYN BRAGG WAS THE LUCKIEST PEER IN THE HOUSE OF LORDS — FOR HE HAD HIS VERY OWN MONSTER TRUCK.

BANANA NO-NO KO'S BONGO

IT WAS nearly expensive handbags at dawn for a Fulchester housewife last week when she came face to face with an uninvited guest in her shopping.

Joyce Bongo, 46, was unpacking a £1.49 bunch of bananas when a huge **CROCODILE** jumped out of the smile-shaped yellow snacks.

BANANAS

"I was terrified. I immediately phoned the police. It must have been 20ft long," she told reporters yesterday.

Speaking for the first time about her Steve-Irwin-like close encounter, she described how the maddened reptile sent saucepans flying as it thrashed violently around her kitchen.

"From the garden, it looked like a giant food mixer full of teeth," she said, coming close to non-crocodile real actual tears. "I just stood there screaming."

AGAIN

While Joyce was being sedated by worried neighbours, specially trained police said "See Ya Later

BANANA DRAMA: The croc which leaped out of Mrs Bongo *(inset)* 's shopping.

Alligator" to the crocodile by letting it out into the street and trapping it under a two-storey pint glass.

Joyce, still 46, is now threatening legal action against the supermarket, Cornerstone's.

"They should check the boxes before they sell them," she fumed.

TO MONTE CARLO

Meanwhile Cornerstone's has apologised to Joyce and offered her a free banana as compensation, but the plucky shopper says this is too little too soon.

"I know my rights," she stormed. "What if it had got into the skirting board? In a few weeks, the whole place would have been infested with crocodiles. I'm going to fight this to the end."

Joyce, 46, is 47 next fortnight.

This isn't the first time an unlucky consumer has taken home something extra from the shops. In 1996 two Egyptian schoolboys came across a goat in a packet of peanuts. The same month a woman from Scotland found a set of bagpipes in a loaf of bread. And famously, on her 70th birthday, the Queen Mother nearly ate a baked bean that had made its way into a tin of dead mice.

BIFFA BACON

HOO, NORSE!.. THE BAIRN'S GOT A BIT SPLINTER IN 'IS FINGER!

AYE! IT'S CANNY DEEP, LIKE

HMM! WELL, AS IT'S ONLY A MINOR INJURY, I'M AFRAID IT WILL BE THREE HOURS BEFORE HE'S SEEN BY A DOCTOR

THREE FUCKIN OOWAZ?

RECEPTION

YES. YOU SEE, SERIOUSLY INJURED PATIENTS TAKE TOP PRIORITY.

BIFF! THUMP! BOOT!

WHACK!

HOO, NORSE!.. THE BAIRN'S GOT A BIT SPLINTER IN 'IS FINGER...

GROAN!

GOLDFISH BOY

AFTER LOSING HIS PARENTS IN A BIZARRE FAIRGROUND ACCIDENT, YOUNG JOHNNY JOHNSON WAS TAKEN IN AND RAISED BY KINDLY GOLDFISH ON THE HOOK-A-DUCK STALL. AFTER SEVERAL YEARS, HE HAD BEEN WON BY FATHER BROWN THE LOCAL VICAR, WITH WHOM HE NOW LIVED.

LOOK WHAT I'VE GOT, GOLDFISH BOY...

...'CALENDAR GIRLS.' IT'S JUST BEEN RELEASED ON DVD

IT'S ALL ABOUT SOME WOMEN'S INSTITUTE MEMBERS WHO RAISE MONEY FOR THEIR LOCAL CHURCH BY POSING NUDE FOR A SAUCY CALENDAR. IT'S A TRUE STORY, APPARENTLY

I'D LIKE TO SEE THE LADIES OF MY CONGREGATION DO THAT

HEH! HEH! NOW TO COP AN EYEFUL OF HELEN MIRREN AS GOD INTENDED

I HOPE YOU GET TO SEE HER NIPS IN THIS ONE. THEY WERE LIKE CHAPEL HATPEGS IN PRIME SUSPECT 3

BUT...

AW, NO! IT'S IN LETTERBOX FORMAT! PAH!

I'LL NOT BE ABLE TO SEE A THING ON THIS LITTLE SCREEN

LORD, WHAT I WOULDN'T GIVE FOR ONE OF THOSE BIG 42 INCH PLASMA TELLIES LIKE THEY'VE GOT IN DIXONS...

...WITH A NEW DVD AND DOLBY PRO-LOGIC SURROUND SOUND SPEAKERS, THEY ONLY COST FIVE GRAND

OH, THIS MIRACLE'S NOT GOING TO HAPPEN, GOLDFISH BOY...

...HE CAN FEED FIVE THOUSAND WITH TWO LOAVES AND FIVE FISH, BUT HE CAN'T FIND FIVE GRAND FOR MY TELLY. I SOMETIMES WISH HE'D MOVED IN LESS MYSTERIOUS WAYS

STILL, THE LORD HELPS THOSE WHO HELP THEMSELVES, THEY SAY...

...HMM! I WONDER IF I COULD KILL TWO BIRDS WITH ONE STONE...

NEXT DAY...

THANK YOU SO MUCH FOR COMING, LADIES

NOT AT ALL, VICAR. THAT'S WHAT THE LOCAL WOMEN'S INSTITUTE IS FOR, HELPING OUT THOSE IN NEED

WELL, SELDOM HAS OUR NEED BEEN SO GREAT, MRS. ARBUTHNOT. I'M AFRAID WE NEED TO RAISE £5,000 FOR A NEW CORK NOTICEBOARD FOR THE CHURCH HALL, AND, AHEM, SUNDRY OTHER ITEMS

AND I'VE DECIDED THAT A CHARITY PHOTOGRAPHIC CALENDAR DEPICTING VARIOUS TABLEAUX OF WOMEN FROM THE BIBLE WOULD BE THE BEST WAY OF RAISING THE MONEY

A SPLENDID IDEA, FATHER. SPLENDID!

YES. I CAN SEE IT NOW... MYSELF AS THE VIRGIN MARY, HEAVY WITH CHILD, MAKING MY WAY ON A DONKEY TO BETHLEHEM. MATTHEW CH. 6 VERSE 8

ERM, YES, MRS. ARBUTHNOT. BUT ACTUALLY I'VE GOT YOU DOWN AS MATTHEW 14, VERSE 6... SALOME DOING A SEXUALLY PROVOCATIVE BELLY DANCE...

...IN THE RIK

VICAR! WHAT ON EARTH ARE YOU SUGGESTING?

COME, COME, MRS. ARBUTHNOT. YOUR BODY IS NOTHING TO BE ASHAMED OF...

...WE ARE ALL MADE IN THE LORD'S IMAGE, YOU KNOW. NAKEDNESS IS A GIFT FROM GOD AND SHOULD BE USED IN THE FURTHERANCE OF HIS GLORY

WHAT'S MORE, I SHALL BE TAKING THE PHOTOGRAPHS MYSELF, AND YOU'VE NOT GOT ANYTHING I HAVEN'T SEEN ON EUROTRASH MANY TIMES

I WON'T DO IT, VICAR

WELL, WHAT ABOUT 2 SAMUEL CHAPTER 11 VERSE 3... ...YOU, AS BATH-SHEBA TEMPTING KING DAVID BY LIFTING YOUR NIGHTIE AND FLASHING YOUR...

FATHER BROWN!

WE HAVE NEVER BEEN SO INSULTED IN ALL OUR LIVES

INDEED. YOUR SUGGESTION IS A DISGRACE

THE VERY IDEA! COME ALONG, LADIES

SLAM!

BUGGER IT!

NEVER MIND, GOLDFISH BOY. I'LL PUT IT TO THE CHURCH KNITTING CIRCLE TOMORROW

I'VE HEARD THAT ONE OR TWO OF THEM PUT IT ABOUT A BIT. THEY MIGHT BE A BIT MORE GAME

Letterbocks

Letterbocks, Viz Comic, PO Box 1PT,
Newcastle upon Tyne, NE99 1PT letters@viz.co.uk

I don't believe in giving to charities which help the blind. It's not as though they're going to see any of the money.

Simon Reety
e-mail

Ronseal Woodstain does exactly what it says on the tin, does it? Funny that. I've looked all over the label and nowhere does it say 'Makes your front door look like an African elephant has wiped its arse on it.'

Steve Edwards,
Welshpool

I'm fed up of fast food restaurant assistants telling me 'Sorry about your weight'. Have they no feelings? Or do they think that just because I'm fat, my skin is made of leather

Dan Halen
e-mail

On the BBC website, I read with interest that some scientists in Australia have discovered the smallest fish known to exist. They've obviously never been to the Britannia Chippy on the Gloucester Road.

Alan J. Thackray
London

The BBC's recent billboard advertisements claim that their internet site is 'the web with knobs on'.

How right they are. Upon viewing the page I was greeted with pictures of Jonathan Ross and Martin Clunes. Hats off to the advertisement team for their accuracy.

Mickey
Blackburn

Children in Need? I don't think so. When our Dave rang the helpline because he needed an MP3 player, they just told him to fuck off.

Mrs B.Rubber
e-mail

If motorists are allowed to demand that speed cameras are painted yellow so they can see them, can I demand that plainclothed policemen be painted a similar bright colour to give me half a chance when I'm trying to break into a house? You can't see the buggers until they're right on you.

Norman Stanley Fletcher
HM Prison, Slade

Never mind small buses and dustbin lorries, what about this little petrol tanker? Beat that.

Cliff Erosion
Leeds

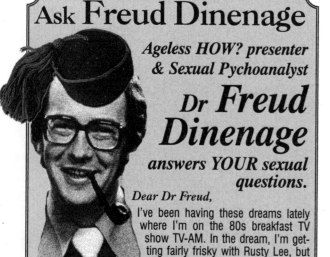

I am convinced that Ant and Dec are the same person. Think about it – have you ever seen them in the same room together?

Dean Franklin
e-mail

So the Home Office is introducing electronic fingerprinting at airports, so that the movements of would-be terrorists can be tracked via a central computer database. Why not extend this technology to electronic face scanning for clowns? No two clowns possess the same facial make-up, and the system could be used to track the movements of would-be paedophiles around the world.

Mr Angel Victorio
e-mail

Children say the funniest things! The other day when my husband's elderly mother was visiting, my 3-year-old son blurted out a real howler, the details of which I unfortunately cannot remember. Well, I don't mind admitting that my face turned bright red after that little speech! Luckily, my mum-in-law soon saw the funny side.

B. Walsh
Dublin

I read that Harold Shipman waited to kill himself until the day after the date that his wife became eligible to claim on a £100 grand insurance policy payable on his death. How very thoughtful and kind. He must have been a lovely man.

Justin Batchelor
e-mail

They say standards are slipping in the police force. Nonsense, I say. My mate is a newsagent and his father got beaten within an inch of his life during a late night robbery. Of the two policemen who attended the crime scene, one asked my mate if he kept *Anglers' Weekly*, while the other perused the top shelf mags and tried to buy six cans of Stella. Let's hear it for our wonderful boys in blue.

AB,
Staffordshire

Whilst Ralf Schumacher was still trapped in the twisted wreckage of his car following his 200mph crash in the US Grand Prix, I was appalled to see his brother Michael continue driving round the track as if nothing had happened. Luckily, he got his priorities sorted out by the next lap, when he took the opportunity to make a "free" pit-stop, filling his

soap dish
with Jo Soap

FANS of multiple murderess Rose West are in for a treat when the killer swaps Cromwell Street for Coronation Street.

Bespectacled Rose will guest star in an episode of the soap, playing Ivy Tilsley's sister Ethel, who emigrated to Australia in the 60s.

A street insider told us: "Rose's character has won the Australian lottery and turns up at Mike Baldwin's factory looking for her long-lost sister. On the way out, she trips over a sewing machine and twists her ankle just as a Health and Safety inspector walks in. It's an hilarious episode."

Security at the Granada studios was tight as the House of Horrors monster was driven to and from Durham prison on the filming days.

Another insider told us: "We had a lot of fun. Rose kept forgetting her lines and cracking up, but we got the scenes in the can in the end."

Ask Freud Dinenage

Ageless HOW? presenter & Sexual Pychoanalyst

Dr Freud Dinenage

answers YOUR sexual questions.

Dear Dr Freud,

I've been having these dreams lately where I'm on the 80s breakfast TV show TV-AM. In the dream, I'm getting fairly frisky with Rusty Lee, but when I pull my manhood out, she lets rip with her trademark laugh. Needless to say, I am very upset in the dream, but then fitness queen Mad Lizzie comes over and I give her a ruddy good seeing to. Am I normal?

Craig Mitchell, Montrose

*Have YOU had any sexual dreams involving breakfast TV presenters, past or present? If so, write in and describe them, in as much detail as possible to Dr Freud and he will analyse them, free of charge. Particularly if they involve Sophie Raworth and Natasha Kaplinski. Feel free to include any diagrams or computer generated images you feel may help Dr Freud's analysis. Send them to Dr Freud Dineage's How Sex Clinic, Viz Comic, PO Box 1PT, Newcastle upon Tyne, NE99 1PT. Dr Freud apologises, but he cannot answer any sex related questions either privately or in his column.

tank with fuel and getting a fresh set of tyres whilst the safety car was out.

Mrs. Ecclescake
Whittlebury

When we were at school, a mate of mine told me he used to wank off over Annalise from *Neighbours*. I never believed him though. Do you think you could ask her politely if she recalls being sprayed with spunk by a teenager from Yeovil, about ten years ago?

Robert Graff
Shepton Mallet

LAME to FAME

Did YOU once have a cup tea with Paul McCartney and John Lennon in a cafe? Did Elvis Presley once stop and ask you for directions? Perhaps you were in a lift when who should get in but Bob Dylan.

Well, we're not interested. Because we're looking for Britain's most piss-poor claim to fame. Here's a selection of some of the piss-poorest in this month's mail bag...

...MY MATE once shagged this bird who had shagged Keith 'Nice fella' Deller, the youngest ever darts World Champion.

Jack Boot, e-mail

...I SOMETIMES chat with a girl in the coffee shop on Portobello Road whose brother is Ringo in The Bootleg Beatles.

Tim Briffa, London

...TWO WEEKS AGO I got married, and guess who was at the wedding? Gabby Tolkien, JRR's nephew, that's who. How do you like them apples, fish face?

Lee Allberry, Evesham

...EX-MANCHESTER United star Brian McClair is my second cousin, once removed. Although I've never met him, I could have got his autograph before I fell out with that side of the family.

Graham Wynn, Lancaster

...WHEN HE WAS a nipper, my dad was taught to whistle by the brother of Paul O'Grady, aka unfunny tranny Lily Savage.

Neil, Birkenhead

If YOU have a Lame to Fame, write in to the usual address and let us know. There's a night out with the sister-in-law of a bloke who once met the sister of the man who wrote 'Blame it on the Boogie' for the poorest we recieve.

TOP TIPS

RECREATE the feeling of time travel by falling asleep on the train and awakening on arrival at your destination. Hey presto, you've arrived in the future!

Geoff Wilson
Nottingham

MEN. Make sure that your lady always gets to sleep in the wet patch by ejaculating into her side of the bed before she gets into it.

Manytrix
e-mail

JULIAN from Anglian Homes. Cover up the mouthpiece on your phone next time you ask your supervisor what to do, and he replies 'make something up.'

Ted Bundy
e-mail

PENPALS. If you and your penpal should fall out, simply send each other empty envelopes.

Fiona
e-mail

OLD people. Next time you start a conversation with

the words 'Of course, it goes without saying…' you can then simply shut up, because whatever you were about to say obviously goes without saying.

Adrian Horsman
Banbridge, Co. Down

LADIES. When invited to a Buckingham Palace garden party, go wearing hair rollers, so that the Queen will think you are going somewhere REALLY important afterwards.

Chris Davies
Email

TEACHERS. Avoid fancying 15-year-old girls in your charge by picturing them engaged in much younger activities, such as sucking large lollipops or frolicking naked in a paddling pool.

Bellester Smith
e-mail

SHOPPERS. If what you wish to purchase is not in stock, inform the assistant that you've come all the way from Stanely on the

No.2 bus. They will take pity on you and have your item materialize out of thin fucking air.

Johnny
e-mail

VETS. A human armpit hair makes a great prosthetic leg for an invalid spider.

Hedgepig
Crewe

MOTHERS. Don't use poisonous shampoos on your children's hair to get rid of headlice. Scare them away using a dinner plate and an anglepoise lamp to cast a terrifying *'Independence Day'* shadow over your child's head.

A. Feather
Caterham

SMARTIES tubes pushed over cats' legs make for a futuristic 'space cat'. For a really space age look, cover the tubes in tin foil as well as your pet's tail. This also works with small dogs and the middles out of kitchen rolls.

Dominic Rickard
e-mail

Miriam's Photo Problem Casebook
Suzie's Boyfriend Worries - Day 3

Suzie has been dating her boyfriend Dave for a year, but recently he has been having problems operating his 35mm camera. She turns to her best friend Claire for advice...

In Suzie's flat...

What's wrong, Suzie? You look worried.

Oh, Claire! It's Dave. I really love him, but whenever he takes a photo of me he puts his thumb in front of the lens...

...either that, or he never gets the focus right and they come out all blurred. I don't know what to do.

Lots of men have that trouble, Suzie...

...come on, have a shower, and we'll go out for a drink.

Shortly...

There! Is that better?

Yes, thanks! I feel...

...Oh, no! He hasn't framed the picture properly... the top of my head is cut off!

In the pub...

I'm sure things will work out between you and Dave, Suzie.

I'm not so sure...

...he's forgotten to turn the red-eye reduction on, **and** he's used too slow a shutter speed causing motion blur...

...Oh, Claire! What am I going to do?

CONTINUES TOMORROW...

107

Raffles

The Gentleman Thug

♪ THUMPA-THUMPA-THUMPA ♪ SET MY HAND UPON THE PLOUGH, MY FEET UPON THE SOD... THUMPA'-THUMPA-THUMPA... ♪

I SAY, RAFFLES OLD BEAN, IT'S A LOVELY MORNING. WHAT SAY WE GO FOR A PEREGRINATION IN THE PARK?

A CAPITAL NOTION, BUNNY OLD CHAP. I'LL JUST GET THE DOG.

I DIDN'T KNOW YOU HAD A DOG, RAFFLES.

WELL, HE'S NOT MINE. I'M JUST LOOKING AFTER HIM FOR A WEEK, BUNNY.

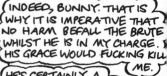

HE BELONGS TO DAVE, 6TH EARL OF BERMONDSEY.

EGAD! HE'S THE NAILSEST PEER IN THE UPPER HOUSE!

INDEED, BUNNY. THAT IS WHY IT IS IMPERATIVE THAT NO HARM BEFALL THE BRUTE WHILST HE IS IN MY CHARGE. HIS GRACE WOULD FUCKING KILL ME.

HE'S CERTAINLY A FINE LOOKING BEAST. WHAT'S HIS NAME?

DARCEY WEAR FOL DE ROL GAYLORD OF PONSONBY...

...OR, IF YOU PREFER, "RIPPER".

HULLO THERE OLD CH...

CAREFUL, BUNNY.

DON'T TOUCH HIM. HE'S EQUALLY CORYBANTIC AS A RETAIL PURVEYOR OF MILLINERY. HE'LL HAVE YOUR FUCKING HAND OFF.

HUDSON, MY VALET, PROFFERED HIM A TRIFLING TICKLE BEHIND THE EARS AND RIPPER GOT HIM BY HIS PHYSIOGNOMY.

I SAY. WHAT A RUM DO THAT MUST HAVE BEEN.

INDEED. I HAD TO LAPIDATE THE LITTLE ILLEGITIMATE IN THE TESTICLES NO FEWER THAN SIX TIMES BEFORE HE COMMENCED TO LEASE HIS VICE-LIKE GRIP ON HUDSON'S FACE.

MY GOD. THE POOR FELLOW! HOW IS HE?

OH, HE'S CAPITAL NOW, BUNNY. I PROCURED HIM A MARROW-BONE FROM THE KITCHEN AND HE CHEERED UP PREVENIGHTLY.

I RATHER MEANT HUDSON, YOUR VALET, RAFFLES.

HOW DREADFUL.

OH, HIM. I'M AFRAID I HAD TO LET HIM GO. HE'D LOST HIS NOSE AND THE GREATER PART OF HIS UPPER LIP IN THE CONTRETEMPS.

INDEED. IT WAS QUITE PUTTING ME OFF MY KEDGEREE IN THE MORNING.

EXCUSE ME, SIR. YOUR HOUND HAS JUST BEFOULED THE FOOTWAY, AND IT HAS ALTOGETHER SPOILED THE PROGRESS OF OUR AMBULATION.

WELL MIGHT I ENQUIRE WHAT THE FUCK YOU WISH ME TO DO ABOUT IT?

YOU SHOULD RUB HIS NOSE IN IT, SIR. THAT SHOULD TEACH HIM A LESSON.

VERY WELL, MADAM.

PUNT!

OOF!

RUB! RUB! RUB!

≈SWOON≈

TOFFEE-NOSED VAGINAS. THEY APPEAR TO BE LABOURING UNDER THE EARNEST MISAPPREHENSION THAT THIS MUNICIPAL AREA IN SOME WAY CONSTITUTES THEIR OWN PERSONAL PROPERTY.

≈GROAN≈

COME ON, RIPPER.

'Des-gusting'

Lynam's movement hits bum note

THE television presenter Desmond Lynam was last night bailed to appear before Bow Street Magistrates after being caught defecating into a piano in Fortnum & Mason's.

The 52-year-old BBC sports anchor was shopping in the exclusive London store when he apparently became gripped with violent stomach cramps. Shocked onlookers then saw him drop his trousers and perform the toilet function under the lid of an £18,000 Bechstein concert grand.

excreted

Posh shopper Lucinda Sopwith-Camel told us: "It was perfectly ghastly. Lynam excreted in full view of the whole music department, and then cleaned himself up with some sheet music. You don't expect that kind of thing from tel-

evision celebrities, and certainly not in Fortnum & Mason."

A sombre-faced Lynam refused to answer reporters' questions as he left Paddington Green police station, and stood behind his solicitor who read a prepared statement. "My client deeply regrets the unfortunate incident which took place yesterday. As the result of a medical condition, Mr Lynam was caught short whilst browsing in the piano department and had no option but to take the action that he did." He added: "He looks forward to the opportunity to clear his name in court."

excorfud

But a Fortnum & Mason's spokesman last night rejected Lynam's version of events. He told us: "Mr Lynam had been acting strangely in the piano department for more than two hours prior to the incident. Security staff had seen him loitering next to several pianos, and had moved him on twice after he began loosening his trousers."

"There are ample lavatory facilities on every floor of Fortnum & Mason's," he added. "Mr Lynam was no further than twenty yards from a toilet when the offence was commited."

A police spokesman confirmed that Lynam had been charged with shitting in a piano in Fortnum & Mason's, and would be appearing before magistrates on Christmas Eve.

Lynam (inset) outside Paddington Green Police station yesterday, and (above) a piano similar to the one he is alleged to have shat in.

Three years ago at Sheffield Crown Court, Lynam pleaded guilty after being caught defecating into an 18th century harpsichord at Chatsworth House. He asked for 148 similar cases to be taken into consideration and was bound over to keep the peace.

¡ Los Showbiz Hombres of the year! **WITH LUCKY DAY, DUSTY BOTTOMS AND NED NEDERLANDER**

ALL THE TOP GOSSIP FROM THE WORLD OF 1920s MEXICAN BORDER SHOWBIZ

wicked whispers

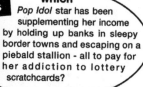 **WHICH** *Pop Idol* star has been supplementing her income by holding up banks in sleepy border towns and escaping on a piebald stallion - all to pay for her addiction to lottery scratchcards?

Deeley wows cantina crowd

AY Caramba! When slinky **Cat Deeley** swaggered through the swinging doors of **El Cantina Voltoro** in Santo Poco, what else could the customers do but make a high-pitched whistling noise and fire their guns in the air? Cat is reported to be dating local evil land baron **El Guapo** and dropped in for a quick glass of fire water on the way to his desert camp. The room fell momentarily silent as Cat downed the ferocious drink in one, shook her head and pounded the bar with her hand.

The regular barfly with the dead eye slapped her on the back, declaring, "This leetle one, she is as strong as a lion." before the entire bar erupted in a riot of mad laughter and spitting.

DOWN IN ONE! Cat shows the locals how it's done.

PONCHO NO-NO'S

There was only one place to be seen yesterday, and that was under a cactus.

All the top names were out snoozing under big hats for yesterday's siesta, but not everybody got it right.

So here's a rundown of the afternoon's big fashion disasters!

¡UH-OH! Veteran TV funnyman **Alan Davies** was caught on the hop when his elaborate new sombrero began attracting flies... So many flies that when he woke up, he couldn't see where he was going and fell down a well!

¡OH-NO! Hollywood film star **Minnie Driver** must have left her clothes sense in her saddle-bag! Her fusty old poncho made her look like a dead horse with a blanket thrown over it to keep the buzzards away!

¡ ARIBA! But here's how it should be done! Arts Minister **Estelle Morris** put the others to shame with a dazzlingly simple rainbow-stripe poncho that drew wolf-whistles from a passing stagecoach! Wow!

SURVEILLANCE TELEGRAPH THE AMIGOS ON SANTO POCO 453 IF *YOU* SPOT A CELEBRITY! and you could win yourself a state-of-the-art Hughes R50 Telegraph Machine

LORRAINE KELLY lying on a flat rock with a rifle waiting for El Diablo Negro to ride past and hoping to collect the bounty! ... **KELLY OSBOURNE** starting a stampede with a pair of castanets ... Hunky **COLIN FARRELL** being rescued from the gallows by one of the **CHEEKY GIRLS** ... **STING** falling off a donkey ... **SADIE FROST** sending **CLAIRE SWEENEY** sliding along the top of the bar with a single punch!

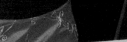

WAR OF TH

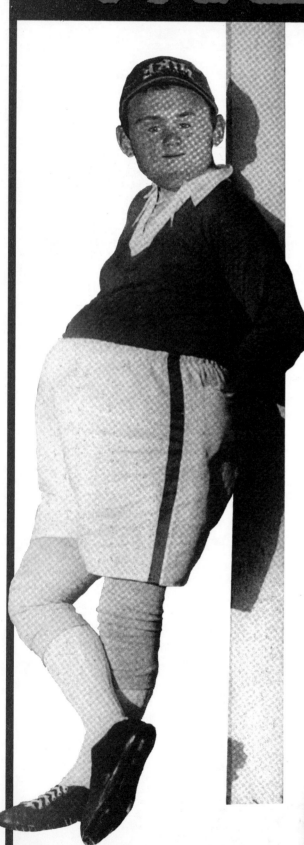

WAYNE ROONEY

SC

As anyone who watched Euro 2004 will testify, Rooney's shooting skills are more than a match for any Wild West gunslinger. Equally at home kicking with either foot - or even his potato-like head - he rarely fails to hit his target, burying the ball in the back of the onion bag every time. Consequently, the Everton and England striker scores impressively in this round.

8 SHAR

At the tender age of 18, Rooney has already notched up a list of footballing achievements which would put any player twice or even three times his age to shame. As the youngest player ever to score a goal for England, his sideboard at home is already groaning under the weight of accolades.

8 FOOTH

Not even Rooney's mother in her most deluded moments would claim that young Wayne is blessed with matinee idol good looks. However, pig-ugliness has proved no bar to Hollywood success for many other footballers, such as Vinnie Jones (Lock, Stock and Two Smoking Barrels), Eric Cantona (Elizabeth) and Nobby Stiles (Predator II). Who knows? Perhaps a glittering film career may yet await the Everton golden boy.

6 HOLLYW

Rooney may never have joined the armed forces, but he has proudly worn England's colours on the battlefields of Europe - the Portuguese football pitches of Euro 2004. He fought bravely against foreign foes for his Queen and country, scoring 4 goals and nearly punching a Frenchman. His performance was every bit as courageous, if not more so, as that of those lads of his own age who went "over the top" in the trenches of World War 1.

7 MILITA

As a teenage professional footballer for Everton and England, Rooney has never won an Academy Award. In fact, he's never even been nominated! Consequently, he scores unimpressively in this section.

5 ACADE

Rooney's no-nonsense name seems to sum up his pugnacious British bulldog spirit. 'Rooney' is Anglo-Saxon for fight, and 'Wayne' is a Christian name exclusively associated with the hardest men in the country. If you don't include Wayne Sleep. Or Wayne Hemingway.

9 HARDN

Typing Rooney's name into the popular Google search engine throws up an impressive score of 76,400 websites all about him. This proves beyond doubt that the fleet-footed Scouser is a hot topic on the world's internet lips. A high-scoring round.

7 INTERNE

Rooney recently gave long-term girlfriend Colleen a £25,000 diamond ring by way of apology after allegedly going with a whore. This touching gesture shows that the soccer star is an incurable romantic at heart. His relationship is as strong as his legendary left boot, and his excellent score in this round reflects this.

8 RELA

His electrifying performances on the field during Euro 2004 led to Wayne being dubbed 'King Rooney' by the British press. His throne was well-deserved, as he slotted goal after goal past hapless foreign keepers, earning his place as the Jewel in the Crown of England's conquering heroes.

7 ROY

Cheeky scally Rooney rarely ventures out in public without first donning his trademark baseball cap. With an estimated volume of less than 2 pints, it's a piece of headwear that can easily contain his genius-level footballing brain, but would struggle to hold a significant quantity of liquid.

0 HAT

It's a spirited try from the 18-year-old footballing wunderkind, but is he the winner? The Hell he is. Beaten and humiliated, he limps off this battlefield as he limped off that football pitch in Portugal. He's let himself down, but worst of all he's let his country down once again.

65 F SC

WAYNES

Liverpudlian charm, Scouse appeal and Merseyside good looks have assured him of a place in the heart of every true red, white and blue England fan? It's time to get off your horse, drink your milk and tot up the scores in our fantastic fun, yet rigorously scientific, test to decide the champion Wayne once and for all.

JOHN WAYNE

...TING 9
Toting his trademark Colt 45 in Westerns such as True Grit, Stagecoach and High Noon, John Wayne never lost a shootout, despite appearing in over 140 films. His unerring aim kept dozens of Hollywood Wild West undertakers working round the clock for over 40 years. What's more, a man's heart is 1000 times smaller than a regulation Association football net, making his shooting skills that much sharper than Rooney's lame efforts.

...AREER 7
A little-known fact about John Wayne is that if his film career had not been a success, he could easily have made his mark in the world of football. Like Rooney he was a teenage sporting prodigy, and in the 20s won a football scholarship to the University of Southern California. However, it was that American fancy dress football, and so his score suffers in this round.

...CAREER 5
Wayne enjoyed great success through nearly four decades on the silver screen. Making his acting debut in 1930's 'Big Trail', he went on to appear in well over 140 feature films, taking countless millions of dollars at the box office. However, 3 years after starring 'The Shootist' in 1976, he succumbed to cancer and his Hollywood career has been on hold ever since. As a result, he makes a surprisingly lacklustre showing in this round.

...NOURS 7
Despite wearing every military uniform from Confederate Cavalry Officer to WWII Marine during his film career, John Wayne never actually served his country. Thanks to his flat feet, he avoided enlistment in the forces, and had to be content with pretending to be a soldier in films such as 'The Sands of Iwo Jima', 'The Longest Day' and 'The Green Berets' instead.

...VARDS 4
John Wayne was awarded the Best Actor prize for his performance in the 1969 blockbuster 'True Grit'. However, for an actor who starred in so many films, a tally of a single Oscar is frankly poor, and his points in this round reflect this.

...F NAME 7
'John Wayne' is undoubtedly a very macho name, but few people know that it's not actually his real name. Born in Iowa in 1907, the actor was actually christened Marion Elspeth Pixie-Frou-Frou Morrison. Sharing the same name as a Yorkshire-based supermarket group is undoubtedly a bit soft, so John Wayne's score suffers accordingly.

...ULARITY 5
A similar search performed on John Wayne throws up a mere 64,900 sites. Such a lack of interest suggests that the late actor is unable to hold his own in these modern technological times. He's an outdated dinosaur, and his score verges on extinction as a result.

...HIPS 6
Serial womaniser Wayne went through wives like a dose of salts, keeping Hollywood vicars busy marrying him to different women an incredible THREE times. He wed final wife Pilar Pallette in 1954, and only managed to remain faithful to her for a mere quarter of a century before he was off down the aisle again... this time in his coffin!

...TLES 6
Despite being admired by many during his long life, John Wayne was only ever accorded the honorary title of Duke. According to snobs' bible Debrett's, Dukes are an amazing 17 times less good than Kings. The cowboy star is easily outclassed by his footballing counterpart in this round.

...CITY 10
The Duke was well known for his 10-gallon hat, a massive stetson which could hold an impressive 80 pints of fluid, such as milk or juice. With his hat capacity easily outstripping Rooney's piddling effort by over 40 times, it's hats off to John Wayne, as he wins this final round.

...AL ...RE 66
John Wayne has showed true grit winning this, the most important shoot-out of his career. Babyface Rooney's reputation lies dead in the dust as the Duke blows the smoke from the barrel of his blazing six-gun. It's time to saddle up and raise two fingers of red-eye to John, the greatest Wayne there has ever been!

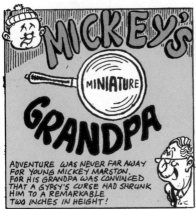

MICKEY'S MINIATURE GRANDPA

ADVENTURE WAS NEVER FAR AWAY FOR YOUNG MICKEY MARSTON. FOR HIS GRANDPA WAS CONVINCED THAT A GYPSY'S CURSE HAD SHRUNK HIM TO A REMARKABLE TWO INCHES IN HEIGHT!

HI MICKEY! I'VE SET UP MY OWN MIDGET-SIZED SHOW-JUMPING COURSE ~ USING A **MOUSE** INSTEAD OF A HORSE!

WATCH ME JUMP OVER THAT PENCIL!

MR MARSTON...

DON'T WORRY, MICKEY, I WON'T GET INJURED. THIS THIMBLE 'RIDING HELMET' IS THE PERFECT FIT FOR MY LITTLE HEAD.

GIDDYUP, DOBBIN!

MR MARSTON, I'M NOT MICKEY. MICKEY IS YOUR GRANDSON, ISN'T HE?

I'M CHERRYL, YOUR CARE ASSISTANT. REMEMBER?

LET'S GET YOU SETTLED BACK IN BED.

I'VE BROUGHT YOU A BOWL OF LOVELY LUKEWARM SOUP FOR YOUR LUNCH.

GASP! I'LL NEVER EAT ALL THAT, MICKEY! THIS BOWL OF SOUP IS LIKE AN OLYMPIC-SIZED SWIMMING POOL TO SOMEONE OF MY TINY STATURE!

JUST EAT WHAT YOU CAN. I'LL BE DOWNSTAIRS SPONGING DOWN YOUR RUBBER SHEETS.

I'LL USE THIS THIMBLE AS A BUCKET TO SCOOP OUT A MORE MANAGEABLE PORTION OF SOUP.

GRUNT! IT'S A BIT HEAVY, THOUGH.

SHRIEK!

I'VE LOST MY FOOTING AND FALLEN INTO THE BOWL!

HELP ME MICKEY! (=GLUB! GLUB!=) I CAN'T SWIM!

(=GLUB! SPLUTTER!=) I'M DROWNING IN SOUP!

PHEW! I MANAGED TO PADDLE TO THE SIDE OF THE BOWL BY USING A CROUTON AS A FLOAT.

NOW TO CLIMB BACK ONTO DRY LAND. UGH! I'M SOAKING!

I'D BETTER GET OVER TO THE FIRE AND DRY OFF. BUT HOW WILL I GET DOWN FROM THE BED?

IT'S LIKE A SHEER CLIFF FACE TO A TINY LITTLE FELLOW LIKE ME.

OHO! I COULD USE THAT DADDY-LONG-LEGS AS A MINIATURE MOUNTAIN RESCUE HELICOPTER

IF I CAN JUST GRAB HOLD OF ONE OF ITS LEGS...

GOT IT! NOW I JUST NEED TO CLING ON TIGHT, AND LET IT CARRY ME DOWN TO THE FLOOR

WE HAVE LIFT-OFF!

THUD!

AW MUM, DO WE HAVE TO GO AND VISIT GRANDPA MARSTON? HE SMELLS OF LINIMENT AND SPITS WHEN HE TALKS.

THAT'S ENOUGH, MICKEY. HE'S VERY OLD. AND YOU KNOW HOW HE LOVES TO SEE YOU.

OH MY GOODNESS! THAT'S THE DOCTOR AT YOUR GRANDPA'S HOUSE.

WHAT CAN HAVE HAPPENED?

I'M TERRIBLY SORRY, MRS MARSTON. I'M AFRAID THAT YOUR FATHER HAS PASSED AWAY.

IT SEEMS HE SUFFERED A FATAL FALL OFF HIS BED, FOLLOWING AN INCIDENT WITH SOME SOUP AND A WINGED INSECT.

(=SOB=) OH DEAR (=SNIFF SNIFF=) POOR OLD DAD (=SNIFF SNIFF=)

THERE, THERE, MRS MARSTON. I'M SURE ITS HOW HE WOULD HAVE WANTED TO GO.

(=SNIFF=) WELL I SUPPOSE I'D BETTER PHONE AN UNDERTAKER AND MAKE THE FUNERAL ARRANGEMENTS.

THERE'LL BE NO NEED FOR THAT, MRS MARSTON...

...THIS **MATCHBOX** WILL MAKE AN IDEAL COFFIN FOR YOUR FATHER'S MINISCULE BODY!

THEN YOU CAN BURY HIM IN THAT PLANT-POT ~ THE PERFECT PINT-SIZED CEMETERY FOR HIS TINY GRAVE!

FRU T. BUNN — THE MASTER BAKER & HIS GINGERBREAD SEX DOLLS

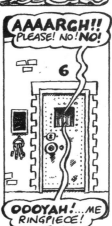

Letterbocks

Letterbocks, Viz Comic, PO Box 1PT, Newcastle upon Tyne NE99 1PT

STAR LETTER

● According to the Discovery Channel, our closest living relatives are chimpanzees. That's bollocks. My closest living relative is my twin brother Dave.

U Helmet, e-mail

● I'm sick of people who confidently claim they are not gay. I took a rather large cock up my arse recently and I didn't like it at all. I *know* I'm not gay, but how can they be sure.

Richard Cheese
Stilton

● I bought 3 bottles of scotch at Tesco the other day, drank it all that night and threw up all over my carpet. It was only afterwards that I noticed that the whisky was in fact 25 years old. No wonder I was sick.

B Johnson
e-mail

● I'm a retired hairdresser, and when I was young, gay was a perfectly good word for homosexual. Now apparently, it's a playground word meaning 'rubbish' or 'not very good'. How much longer are we going to stand around and watch as our words are hijacked by the schoolchild community.

Quentin Crispacket
London

● How come it was all well and good for Willy Wonka to lure children into his factory on the promise of free chocolate, but when my mate who works at Cadbury World tried the same thing, he was sacked and put on the sexual offenders register?

Ian Chocolington-Gore
e-mail

● I recently came across this photo of a much younger Mickey Rooney and a disturbingly much older Elvis Costello. Perhaps one of your readers could explain this apparent shift in the space time continuum.

Greg Chown
Toronto

● 'People treat you as you allow them to treat you' lectures my mum whenever I visit her for a cup of tea. How the prisoners at Guantanamo Bay must wish they had such a wise mother.

David Thompson
e-mail

● Last night I went to the loo whilst listening to my personal stereo. As I got my old boy out and started to pee, the theme tune to *Rocky* started playing. Never before have I felt so manly.

Dom R
e-mail

● I think parachutes used by paratroopers should be made from the same material as the edible knickers you can get from Ann Summers. When they land on the battlefield, they could quickly eat their parachutes so as not to divulge their position to the enemy.

Barry Fox
United Kingdom

● Whilst eating in a restaurant last week, I was disgusted to see two very elderly women walking arm in arm to the lavatory, quite clearly on their way to indulge in lesbian sexual intercourse. They were so excited they could barely stand up. You would have thought that they had enough hair around their mouths at that age, but obviously not. I'm not homophobic, but in a restaurant full of children, I would expect the older members of our society to behave more responsibly than that.

Tom
Hebden Bridge

● 'Let Me Entertain You' sang monkey-faced crooner Robbie Williams. Okay, Robbie, in your own time.

Emord Nilap
Dover

● I recently found some pictures of my mate's bird taken for their personal use. However, the shots were tame in the extreme. Could any of your readers tell me how to get them to shoot some great filth without letting them know I went through their house?

Geoff Mills
e-mail

● Vernon Kay owes me £5 for the Tyson v Bruno fight on Pay-per-View in 1995. Other readers beware if he comes round to watch Pay-per-View TV.

Mez
Stockport

● I was in the pub the other day and I noticed that whilst my Bensons said 'Smoking Kills' on the box, my mate's Regals merely said they would 'Seriously Harm You'.

● Yet another example of one rule for one and another rule for the rest of us.

P Kershawhouse
e-mail

● My family are usually very helpful financially most of the time. Recently, however, I had to buy a new tyre for my car which cost £77. My dad gave me £50 towards it, and my wispy chinned old nan gave me a tenner. The only problem is, I'm still £17 short. Some family they turned out to be.

N Body
e-mail

● If you are ever bored one Sunday afternoon, why not take a laxative followed by an imodium tablet and see which one wins. I can assure you, the tension is unbearable.

Andy Southern
e-mail

● A few weeks backwhilst in the vicinity of Holborn tube station, I saw a 3-legged dog eating from a chunky pool of vomit while some tramps looked on laughing. Have any *Viz* readers witnessed a more depressing scene?

John Ferguson
e-mail

● My grandma always used to tell me 'never put all your eggs in one basket.' However, on a recent trip to a supermarket, I had to make 12 trips to the checkout to pay for a dozen eggs. Then the checkout girl had the cheek to tell me they didn't sell individual eggs.

J Patrick
Sheffield

● In my opinion, today's sex maniacs have taken their perversion too far. These days it's all paedophiles and serial rapists. In my day, sex maniacs like Cosmo Smallpiece confined their activities to leering at

ladies' cleavages, stealing the odd bra from a washing line and almost touching a woman's buttocks when she was getting on a bus. What about a campaign to bring back the good old-fashioned British sex maniac.

T Pottersbar
Potters Bar

● I've seen some pretty small tankers, bin lorries and buses in the last few pages, but this fire engine must take the biscuit.

Tieran Welch
Leicester

● After WigWatch, how about SpecSpotter? I'll start the ball rolling with Councillor Eileen Kinnear from the London Borough of Harrow. She must have mighty strong ears.

Mad Eddy
London

● Why is it that posters asking whether we want to earn an extra income of £500-£1000 per week are always in the back window of really shit B-reg Nissan Bluebirds?

Ted Cunterblast
e-mail

...Anyone for Tenuous?
Another selection of your pathetic 'Lames to Fame'

...I used to play in the same football team as a bloke who once caught Simon le Bon's (out of Duran Duran) dog after it escaped from his big house.

Peter Hurley, e-mail

...one of my wife's parents' neighbours brags about the fact that he once artexed a ceiling for Rick Astley's mum. Impressively piss poor.

Chris McDonald, e-mail

...I once got off with a girl who lived across the road from the boy who played Adrian Mole on the telly.

Steve Hunt, e-mail

...before he retired, my dad was a dental aneasthetist, and he once anaesthetised the wife of one of the Chuckle brothers. Unfortunately, he can't remember whether it was Paul or Barry's wife.

Daniel Hobson, e-mail

Have you got an unimpressive connection to the glitzy world of showbiz? Perhaps your dad used to drink in the same pub as Duncan 'chase me' Norvell. Or perhaps you went to buy some fags for Ian McCulloch out of Echo and the Bunnymen. Write to 'Anyone for Tenuous, at the usual Viz comic address.

APOLOGY

In the next issue of Viz we will publish an article entitled 'Bamber's Ring Sting Heaven' in which we will accuse University Challenge host Bamber Gascoigne of inserting wasps into his anus in order to achieve sexual pleasure.

With foresight, we realise that this article will be in very poor taste and will be upsetting and embarrassing to Mr Gascoigne and his family. We accept that our allegations will have no grounds whatsoever in truth and we apologise for any distress which will be caused.

Olym-Pick *of the* Post

ATHENS 2004

...The British Olympic effort at Athens cost the taxpayer £190 million, and garnered a total of 30 medals. And we're supposed to be impressed? That's almost £6 million per medal. In the trophy shop down the road you can get a little cup with a snooker player on the top for £2.99. The money wasted in Athens would have bought one of these lovely trophies for every man, woman and child in Britain. Surely that would have been a better use of the money as we would all have been winners. except Paula Radcliffe.

John Shuttlecock,
Poole

...Everyone is saying that the Olympic silver medal winner Amir Khan has 'put Bolton on the map'. This is rubbish, as I have a road atlas from 1979 and Bolton is very clearly marked on it.

Clare Hobley,
Manchester

...I could barely contain my excitement when I saw that one of the events in this

year's Olympic games was the women's snatch competition. Imagine my disappointment when I sat down to watch the competition and it turned out to be a bunch of muscly east-european boilers lifting weights. Still, a wank's a wank.

Jez Gee,
Leeds

...I reckon some of the runners in the Olympic games were cheating. By taking the distance and dividing by the time shown at the bottom of the screen, it was clear to see that the people winning the races were secretly running faster than everybody else. Surely the Olympic officials should be wise to this trick by now and put a stop to it. If everyone ran at the same speed it would be a much fairer race and the fastest runners would not have an unfair advantage.

Melvyn Wright,
e-mail

...Why is it that runners with artificial legs in the Paralympics are slower than those with real legs in the proper Olympics? *The Six Million Dollar Man* had two pretend legs and he went like shit off a shovel.

T Bonesteak,
Wales

...I was very impressed with the effort put in by the British team at this year's Athens olympics, and I would like to help

them prepare in some way for Beijing in 2008. To this end, I have installed a sandpit in my back garden and would like to make it available to the women's beach volleyball team for practice.

M Day,
Leeds

...I would like to thank the organisers of the Athens Olympics for their thoughfulness in providing bikini-clad cheerleaders during intervals in the ladies' beach volleyball competition. In Sydney, I found I lost my erection whenever a time-out was called. Thanks to the cheerleaders this year, I was able to remain fully tumescent throughout the game.

P Fibreboard
Prestatyn

...We may not have wone many medals in Athens, but should peanut smuggling ever become an Olympic event, Sharon Davies will surely take double gold. Phwoar!

Rev. J Foucault
Truro

ROGER MELLIE THE MAN ON THE TELLY

123

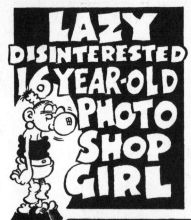

MEDDLESOME RATBAG

KISS IN THE KINGDOM of ROBOT ANTS

OUTRAGEOUS ROCK 'N' ROLL BAND KISS WERE ON A HIKING TOUR OF THE LAKE DISTRICT

ANTIQUES AS THEY WALKED THROUGH THE LITTLE VILLAGE OF BARNTON

LET'S CHECK OUT THIS INTERESTING LOOKING ANTIQUE SHOP, GUYS

SAY — THIS IS A FUNNY OLD POCKET WATCH

LET'S WIND IT UP AND SEE IF IT WORKS

BUT WHEN PAUL WOUND UP THE WATCH, SOMETHING REMARKABLE OCCURRED

WHAT'S GOING ON? WE'RE BEING PULLED INTO SOME KIND OF TIME VORTEX!

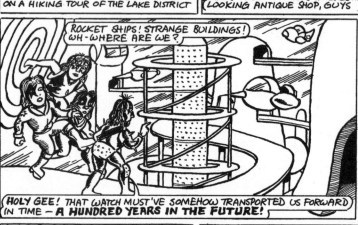

ROCKET SHIPS! STRANGE BUILDINGS! WH-WHERE ARE WE?

HOLY GEE! THAT WATCH MUST'VE SOMEHOW TRANSPORTED US FORWARD IN TIME — A HUNDRED YEARS IN THE FUTURE!

LOOK, GENE — GIANT ROBOT ANTS!

YES. I EXPECT THE HUMAN RACE BECAME EXTINCT, LEAVING THESE GIANT ROBOT ANTS TO RULE THE EARTH

COME WITH US, HUMANS — YOU ARE UNDER ANT ARREST!

UNDER ARREST? BUT WHAT HAVE WE DONE WRONG?

IN OUR NIGHTMARISH FUTURE WORLD OF ROBOTIC ANT-LIKE CONFORMITY, ALL DISPLAYS OF OUTRAGEOUS BEHAVIOUR ARE ILLEGAL

DRESSING OUTLANDISHLY AND STICKING YOUR TONGUE OUT ALL THE TIME ARE STRICTLY FORBIDDEN — AND PUNISHABLE BY **DEATH**!

KISS WERE TAKEN BY ROCKET SHIP TO THE ROBOT ANT KING'S PALACE

AND YOU HAVE BEEN FOUND GUILTY OF FAILING TO ABIDE BY OUR NARROW-MINDED SOCIAL CONVENTIONS.

DO YOU HAVE ANYTHING TO SAY BEFORE I HAVE YOU EXECUTED?

WELL LOOK — SURELY IT'S BETTER TO JUST LIVE AND LET LIVE

AFTER ALL, IT'D BE A DULL OLD WORLD IF WE WERE ALL THE SAME.

THE ROBOT ANT KING LOOKED THOUGHTFUL HMM. THERE IS TRUTH IN WHAT YOU SAY, HUMAN.

I SEE NOW THAT CONFORMITY IS A BAD THING AFTER ALL — WE SHOULD ALL EXPRESS OURSELVES AS INDIVIDUALS INSTEAD. PERHAPS YOU COULD HELP US TO DO THIS?

WELL, WE COULD HOLD A ROCK CONCERT — EH GUYS?

ALRIGHT!

KICK ASS!

AND THAT EVENING IN THE KING'S PALACE

I WANNA ROCK AND ROLL ALL NITE...

SOON THE TIME HAD COME FOR THE FOUR CHUMS TO RETURN BACK TO THE PRESENT DAY

SO LONG, KISS — AND THANKS FOR EVERYTHING

KEEP ROCKIN', GUYS!

I TRUST YOUR VISIT TO MY LITTLE SHOP HAS BEEN AN INTERESTING EXPERIENCE, GENTLEMEN

INTERESTING? PHEW! I SHOULD SAY SO!

MAYBE YOU'D LIKE TO BUY THIS PAIR OF **ANT**-LERS, OR ONE OF THESE CROISS-**ANTS**

NO THANKS! I THINK WE'VE HAD **ENOUGH** "ANT" THINGS FOR ONE DAY!

HA HA HA HA!

MAJOR MISUNDERSTANDING

Letterbocks

Letterbocks, Viz Comic, PO Box 1PT, Newcastle upon Tyne NE99 1PT *letters@viz.co.uk*

STAR LETTER

IF ANYONE is in any doubt as to who it was who shouted 'Oi you. You're a fucking prick you are' to the Lord Mayor of Salford at the end of the recent Swinton Lions vs Sheffield Eagles League 2 match, it was me.

R Harvey, Swinton

TOP MARKS to the designer of this toy catalogue, who managed to slip these enormous bubble genitals into his publication.

Olly Driscoll
Bryants Bottom, Bucks

TODAY'S paper carried a luridly-illustrated article reporting that, during a recent episode of *The Farm* on Channel 5, Debbie McGee had been shown closing her eyes and gritting her teeth whilst sponging the smegma off a horse's penis. This struck me as ironic, since *(The remainder of this letter has been omitted on legal advice)*

R McAllister
Sunbury

WHATEVER the moaning heart lefties and the bleeding minnies say, it is quite right that

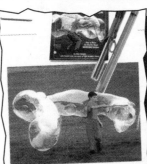

Unbelievable Bubbles

How to make the world's most unbelievable bubbles – 6ft high and 4ft wide! With this 72 page book you can become a world expert on bubbles and even make a bubble within a...

John Lennon's killer Mark Chapman has been refused parole once again. He may have spent three times as long behind bars as any other murderer, but this is only fair as his victim had co-written seventeen No.1s with the Beatles, and had topped the charts a further three times in his own right. Add to this Lennon's further impressive tally of fifteen lesser top ten hits both as a member of the Fab Four and a solo artiste, and I think it is clear that Chapman should remain caged until 2014 at the earliest. Let's face it, he has nobody but himself to blame. Had he decided to shoot Chesney Hawkes, whose ironically titled single *'The One and Only'* was his one and only record to make it into the top twenty, he would be a free man today.

B Rice
Linton-on-Ouse

THESE disabled people can't have it both ways. Half the time they're running Marathons in their wheelchairs and playing basketball at the Paralympics, then in the next breath they're complaining because they can't get into TopShop without a ramp. Come on, disableds, it's make your mind up time – which is it to be?

Major A Hepscott-Farthingale
Berkshire

WHEN people talk about David Beckham, they always say that

he's a brilliant footballer but thick as two short planks. You never hear anyone saying that Stephen Hawking is a genius, but shite at football, do you?

Nick Jones
Sheffield

WHILST buying an air ticket recently, I was told that the price had risen due to a fuel surcharge. You would have thought that by now the airlines would be smart enough to include the price of fuel in their ticket price calculations.

Gooba
email

'THAT BOY has too much time on his hands!' my mum exclaimed. I had to laugh, since I was wearing two wrist watches AND was lying on the pavement with my entire upper body pinned to the ground under a grandfather clock my dad had dropped on me from an upstairs window!

KJ Murphy
email

I RECENTLY saw a documentary on the mistreatment of Afghanistan's dancing bears and how charity funding is coming to their aid. I think some of the money should be spent on lessons, because all they seem to do is stand there and shake.

Gipper
New Zealand

THE LAST time I spent 2 hours swerving all over a Greek road before collapsing on the kerb in a tearful heap, I'd had a pint of ouzo and a bad lamb curry. If that's how Paula Radcliffe prepared for the biggest race of her career, then she's only got herself to blame.

Adam Walker
email

Could God Being an Astronaut Spread AIDS in our Schools?

SCIENCE REVEALS SHOCK NEW DAILY MAIL CODE

MATHEMATICIANS at top boffin coffin Oxford University have uncovered a secret code in the pages of the *Daily Mail.*

Close study of the text has shocked the egghead community – revealing a series of cogent, legible messages, cunningly hidden within the rambling paragraphs of the unreasonable right-wing rabbit hutch liner.

LABORATORY

Dr Jonathan Arms and Dr Rebecca Sh, the authors of the research, which is published in this month's *Science* magazine, say that they first noticed the phenomenon after staring blankly for several hours at a single *Daily Mail* story under laboratory conditions.

EXCLUSIVE

"The journalist seemed to be blaming asylum seekers for him not liking the winning entry for the Turner Prize," Dr Arms explains. "We just couldn't make head or tail of it. But then I thought of just reading every 50th letter."

"And there it was," says Dr Sh. "A secret message – 'HELP HELP I AM AFRAID OF EVERYTHING'."

CONSERVATORY

Astonished by their findings, the pair continued and uncovered the tear-jerking **"DESPITE MY COM-FORTABLE LIFESTYLE I AM BIZARRELY JEALOUS OF THE POOR AND NEEDY"** woven into an otherwise senseless Lynda Lee Potter piece about babysitting; the words **"I DON'T TRUST ANY-BODY"** in a seemingly unintelligible article on why the new breed of working mums can have it all; and the phrase **"COLOUREDS WILL EAT MY CHILDREN"** threaded through a week's worth of Fred Bassett cartoons.

Scholars have looked for sense in the *Daily Mail* for thousands of years, but it is only in the last two decades that computers have made the text searches inevitable.

LIBERALDEMOCRATORY

The discovery of the so-called *Daily Mail* code has been poohpoohed by Fleet Street. "This is old wives' hat," said Piers Morgan last night. "You can find the same so-called codes in the *Daily Telegraph* and *FHM* if you look hard enough."

But excitement about the findings is running high, with academics excited at the first evidence of a guiding intelligence behind the newspaper. A book about the discovery, called simply *The Daily Mail Code* is expected to top both the book and R&B single charts on release. It will be serialized in the *Daily Mail* starting on Monday, followed by a week-long series on how reading the book can give you cancer.

I HAVE managed to avoid weekly shopping trips with the wife for three years now, giving a different excuse each time. That's over 150 excuses the daft bat's fallen for so far. Can anyone beat that?

Big Willie
email

AFTER watching *Scrapheap Challenge* the other day, I wondered why the A-Team have never entered. With their unrivalled skills at turning a pile of shite into an armoured personel carrier, they'd be sure to win every week.

Flippy
email

HOW ABOUT a new section, possibly called 'Crappy Choppers', highlighting the entertaining world of ill-fitting dentures? Here's what looks like a cracking set to get the ball rolling.

Vic Flange
Fircombe

WHO SAYS the Iraq war is a disaster for the Americans? I've just learned that 1000 US servicemen have died there, but that they have killed 12000 of their opponents. That's just like leading 12-1, and it's an away fixture too.

B Beaumont
Peterborough

WOMEN'S athletics is boring. So from now on, I think they should just give the medals out to the birds with the biggest tits. That would soon wipe the smile off Kelly Holmes's face.

Dean
email

WHAT'S ALL this hype about edible underwear, then? I've been married to my missus for 25 years and I don't even eat her cooking, so I'm sure as fuck not going to munch on her knickers.

Chris Welsh
email

THE other day I saw a blind guy walking down the street with his absolutely stunning girlfriend. What a waste. Why can't he go out with a munter like my missus instead and I'll have his? After all, it's all the same to him..

Gary Beergut
email

I WISH I'd sent this photograph to *'Private Eye'*. They pay £10 for stuff like this, not just a shite pencil.

Colin Brown
Grantham

TOP TIPS

LAMES to FAME

Craig Charles once called me over to his car and asked me to put an empty lager bottle in the bin for him.
Vincent Blood, Bournemouth

Jet from Gladiators once crashed into the back of my brother's car and exchanged insurance details with him.
James Gibbons, e-mail

A mate from uni said he knew a bird who once noshed off Rolf Harris in the back of a taxi.
M Bates, Scarborough

Neil Kinnock once pushed in front of me in the ticket office queue at Ealing Broadway Station.
Sophie Wood, email

I recently had breakfast with the man who embalmed Rod Hull.
Dave, Durham

Have YOU got a tenuous link to a famous person? Perhaps your brother once held James Gallway's flute case while he signed autographs outside a theatre in Sheffield, or maybe you met a man from Middlesbrough whose friend receives free bacon sandwiches on condition that he doesn't reveal potentially world-shattering information he knows about Kevin Keegan. Write in and let us know – there's supposedly £10 for every one we print.

CAR owners. Dissuade humorous neighbours from saying 'you can do mine next!' when you're cleaning your car by keeping a hammer in your pocket and starting to batter your windscreen when you see them approaching.
Geoff Owens, e-mail

SAVE money on expensive telephone sex lines. Simply send a text message of unadulterated filth to your own landline. Hey presto! The automatic BT text reader will then repeat back the grot of your own choice to your own front room in husky female tones.
Ian Cramphorn, Trousers

MICHAEL PARKINSON. Take your thorny-issue-avoiding interview style to its ultimate conclusion by inviting Osama Bin Laden onto your show and asking him for funny anecdotes about life on the road.
G Dyke, On his Bike

MOTORISTS. When stopped by the police for speeding or driving dangerously, always indignantly point out that they could better spend their time arresting 'proper' criminals. I haven't tried it myself, but I'm sure they'd see your point and let you off with a warning.
Matt Greatorex, e-mail

HAMMER nails through a cricket ball and roll it around in fallen leaves. Hey presto! An Autumn snowball. Cheap and great fun for the kids.
Matt Greatorex, Again

BANGING two pistachio nutshells together gives the impression that a very small horse is approaching.
Nigel Austin, e-mail

STUDENTS. When asked to write a 3000 word essay, simply draw 3 pictures, as they are worth 1000 words each.
Peter E, e-mail

RURAL affairs ministers. Avoid wasting eggs in public by driving to public functions in a large frying pan.
Harry the Lung, e-mail

MORRISSEY. Stop chirping on about the USA and capitalism in your songs when a) you live over there and b) you go on chat shows just to promote your new album you fucking charlatan.
The Jones Boy, Chesterfield

ATTENTION shandy drinkers. I've found that mixing Kaliber and Hooch makes a fantastic 'reverse shandy'.
Big Heed, Maidenhead

GAMBLERS. For a new gambling opportunity, try sending a £50 note to yourself by Royal Mail.
Chris, London

HOME decorators. Use a roller in each hand and halve your painting time.
B&Q, Swallwell

TOWN planners. Confuse commuters and pensioners by calling new developments 'Sorry this bus is not in service'.
Martin Rafferty, Nottingham

FORMULA one fans. Recreate the excitement of your favourite sport by threading coloured beads onto a string, pulling it taut and lowering one end. For added authenticity, single beads can be used for practice, qualifying etc.
Colin Harrison, Glasgow

TV NEWS reporters. Intersperse your interviews with footage of yourself nodding like a twat. This will help viewers appreciate that what's being said is important and correct.
A Quinn, London

INTERIM governments. Avoid coalition forces overstaying their welcome by yawning loudly and saying you have an early start in the morning.
Hamid Karzai, e-mail

PARENTS. Avoid throwing the baby out with the bath water by using an ordinary kitchen sieve or some chicken wire loosely attached to the bath.
Mrs Peggy Sarsons, Oldham

KEEP an empty bottle of milk in your fridge in case someone wants black coffee or even tea.
Richard Hawkins, e-mail

Our Teacher's a Walnut

BLAINE

They're the two undisputed heavyweights of the TV Magic World with CVs which would make any other conjuror green with envy. In the red corner stands David Blaine, the occult American whose mysterious feats defy all rational explanations. In the blue corner is Britain's Ali Bongo, the fez-wearing shaman whose magical powers are said to rival those of Merlin himself.

V

From Pole to Pole and Equator Equator, from the top of Everest to bottom of the Marianas Ocean trench, there's just one questi on everybody's lips. Which o of these wand-wielding w ards is the greatest? Now, for t first time ever, Blaine and Bongo st into the Magic Circle and fight it c over 7 rounds to decide once and for which one is the most magic-est.

Whether he's biting through a coin, sitting in a perspex box for a few weeks or staring into a girl's eyes and guessing what card she's thinking about, Blaine's spells are never less than mind-blowing. Even Haitian voodoo witch-doctors were left scratching their shrunken heads in amazement when he turned up on their island, bit through a coin and guessed what card they were thinking about. Where his magical powers come from, nobody knows. But one thing's for certain, battling Blaine has come out fighting in the first round.

Blaine is known as the Casanova of conjuring because of his success at casting his spell over women. When he was in his perspex box there was never any shortage of girls willing to flash their assets at him, and his lovelife when not dangling off Tower Bridge is even more enviable. Amongst the notches on his magical bedpost, Blaine numbers singer Fiona Apple, supermodel Josie Moran and even children's author Madonna. And once he gets the ladies back to his Gramercy Park pad, you can bet your boots he doesn't saw them in half. That's right, he fucks them...up their fannies!

From Merlin to Gandalf, from Doug Henning to Jesus, all of history's greatest magicians have had one thing in common - abundant facial hair. However, even after 40 days in a box without shaving, the best Blaine could muster was a wispy bumfluff moustache and beard that would have made any self-respecting 12-year-old cringe with embarrassment. Sadly for the American, his risible facial fuzz shaves valuable points off his score.

Not only has Blaine re-written the rules of magic, he's also re-written the laws of gravity. After carefully positioning his audience, checking several times over his shoulder that they're in exactly the right position for the illusion to work, he apparently rises a couple of inches above the pavement. Even gravity's inventor, the great Isaac Newton, would be unable to explain the phenomenon unless he was watching from a slightly different angle. Consequently, the statesider floats like a butterfly, and scores highly.

Look up the word 'cool' in the Oxford English Dictionary and you'll find just one word - David Blaine! The US star kept New York crowds spellbound in 2000 when he had himself encased in a giant block of ice for over a year, lowering his core body temperature to an amazing 4 degrees centigrade!

Whilst publicising his 'Above the Below' spectacle, Blaine stunned a London press conference by slicing his ear off with a borrowed pen-knife. Amazingly, the next time he appeared in front of photographers a few days later, the ear had miraculously grown back!

Whilst performing his street magic tricks, Blaine shambles along the sidewalk in a pair of dusty, beat-up sneakers which are flat as a kipper's dick. With the best will in the world, not even his best friends could describe these shoes as curly, and as a result he ends the bout on a low-scoring final round.

Blaine has put up a good fight, but in the end his lack of experience shows through, and the young American finds himself well and truly on the ropes. He could have been a contender, but in the end he just doesn't have the bottle...glass...glass...bottle to make the grade in the world of topflight magic.

8	*Seconds out... Round 1* **SPELLS**	8
9	*Seconds out... Round 2* **SUCCESS WITH THE LADIES**	3
5	*Seconds out... Round 3* **FACIAL HAIR**	7
7	*Seconds out... Round 4* **LEVITATION**	6
8	*Seconds out... Round 5* **COOLNESS**	3
7	*Seconds out... Round 6* **EAR GROWING**	8
0	*Seconds out... Round 7* **CURLINESS OF SHOES**	10
44	**REFEREE'S DECISION**	45

Nick Cave and the bad seeds

Oh no.

Oh God.

My cress has failed.

That's the last time I buy seeds off that market.

BONGO

The British contender's powers are no less spectacular than Blaine's. He regularly leaves audiences at *Crackerjack* and the *Basil Brush Show* gasping in disbelief as he produces a confused rabbit from a top hat, or transforms a tightly scrunched up foam ball into three slightly smaller scrunched up foam balls. His mastery of arcane dark arts performing such spells as Pompoms Galore and Tricky Tumblers would have had even magical beast Aleister Crowley quaking with awe. As a result, he matches Blaine blow for blow in this round.

Pulling rabbits out of hats may come easily to Bongo, but pulling women has proved a little more difficult. Whilst his tricks hit the headlines, his lovelife has maintained a low profile. He has rarely, if ever, spent the weekend dancing with a bevy of topless pneumatic blondes by the swiming pool at Hugh Hefner's Playboy mansion. Names such as Jodie Marsh, Jordan and Victoria Silvstedt are unlikely to feature in Ali's little black book. In fact, it is widely believed that Bongo's bedpost boasts just a single, solitary notch - that of his wife of 52 years, Mrs Ada Bongo.

The same cannot be said of Ali Bongo. The British magic man's luxurious, drooping mandarin moustache is surely the envy of every chinaman from Peking to Beijing, whilst his bushy eyebrows and sideburns grow so vigorously that they could almost have been drawn on hastily with his wife's mascara pencil. Like Samson in the Bible, many believe that Bongo's magical powers reside in his facial hair and could be lost if his moustache got wiped off with a flannel.

During his many appearances on *Crackerjack* and *The Basil Brush Show*, Bongo has been known for his lively, bouncing stage style. However, despite hopping from foot to foot throughout his act, he has never thwarted gravity and every time he leaps into the air he comes back down to earth with a resounding bump. Unlike Blaine, the Pongolian magus remains sadly subject to the laws of physics, and therefore retires to his corner bruised at the the end of this round.

As a pensioner, Bongo qualifies for the government's cold weather heating allowance, so it's unlikely he'll be particularly cool this winter. In fact, sat on the sofa in front of his 3 bar fire and wearing his trademark hat, poncho and ladies' tights, the octogenarian magic man should comfortably fend off hypothermia.

Although unlike Blaine he has never cut his ear off, Bongo's powers of auricular regeneration are no less impressive. Like all elderly men, his ears are probably growing at an alarming rate and may soon get too big to fit down the sides of his face.

They may not be the height of fashion, but when it comes to curliness, Bongo's footwear is "da bomb!" In fact, his trademark slippers are so curly that if they were bananas, the EEC would try to ban them! Ali's curly shoes end the match by landing a ten point knockout haymaker square on his opponent's chin.

Hey, presto! Ali is the greatest! The British champ wins, sleight of hands down! Bongo's superior sorcery spells the end of Blaine's title hopes. Thanks to his magic performance over 9 rounds, he pulls a fantastic win out of the hat and takes up his rightful place as the undisputed magicest man in the World.

Well Knock Me Down! with A. Feather

Arriving for her wedding in 1964, Scarborough bride-to-be Brenda Allsopp could only look on in horror as the clifftop crumbled away in front of her, plunging the church containing her marriage ceremony 300 feet into the sea below, never to be seen again.

Forty years later, whilst on a fishing holiday in Australia, Brenda hooked a blue whale and hauled it up onto the dock. Upon slitting it open, she was stunned to find what looked like a church inside the beast's stomach. Her surprise turned to outright amazement when she opened the door...to find her own wedding - including the vicar, her husband-to-be and all her guests - waiting patiently inside!

Pensioner Albert Hardwick could not believe his eyes when he bought a punnet of strawberries at his local market in Aukland, New Zealand. For there, on the top of the pile, was the exact same strawberry that had been stolen from off his plate by a cheeky seagull during a childhood picnic in Kent, England, when he was just 5 years old.

How the fruit had retained its freshness during its 80-year, 12,000 mile odyssey is a mystery that may never be solved. But one thing's for certain - Albert wasn't going to let it get away a second time. He ate it straight up!

Illinois office worker Doreen Margolyes couldn't believe her luck when she logged onto an astrology website on her computer. A flashing window appeared, informing her that she was the millionth visitor to that site and inviting her to enter a prize draw to win $50,000.

But her amazement turned to incredulity just ten minutes later when she visited a teddy bear collecting website, only to find she was the millionth visitor to that page too!

Mathematicians have calculated that the odds against the same person being the millionth visitor to two websites is over 1000 billion to 1. That's the same chance as being struck by lightning 100 times... every day... for your entire life!

Arthur Feather

Arthur Feather is the Professor of Strange Facts at Oxford University

the BUSTY ALIENS

Paul Palmer

PLEASE ACCEPT THIS FLAG OF OUR UNITED NATIONS AS A SYMBOL OF OUR GOOD INTENT.

LET ME SAY THAT ON BEHALF OF ALL THE NATIONS OF OUR PLANET EARTH ...THAT... ER ...

COUGH! AHEM!!

TAP! TAP!!

I THINK YOU'LL FIND MY EYES ARE UP HERE!

AHEM!

BLUSH!

TAP!

SPOILT BASTARD

VETERINARY FINANCIAL SERVICES

138

No Nudes is Good News

Cross undressers ~ tranny nudists frolic on Dullswater beach, yesterday

RESIDENTS of a genteel Dorset coastal town are hopping mad about a new nudist beach which has opened on the seafront. And well they might be - because the saucy beach is reserved for gender-bending *TRANSVESTITES!*

Leading the campaign seeking to close the secluded private beach at Dullswater is local headmaster Olwyn Todd, who says that though nudists are welcome in his town, cross-dressing is a step too far.

"We have several naturist and nudist beaches here, and naked tourism is a big part of the local economy, but we really have to draw the line somewhere. What would happen if a child were to look down from the cliff path and see men dressed as women, prancing in the surf, as naked as the day they were born?"

all-night cabaret

And it's not just the ordinary sort of man who might feel comfortable taking off women's clothing who is getting the community in a palaver. The popularity of the

Naked TVs get Locals' Knickers in a Twist

resort is spreading, attracting top drag acts from all over the country, undressed to the nines for all night cabaret at the water's edge.

"Only last night, I came down to the sea to walk my dog, and was confronted by a crowd of nude, hairy men cheering on another nude hairy man miming to Shirley Bassey," says Todd. "It startled the animal so much that he's refused to give milk ever since."

24-hour all that jazz

And anti-transnudist campaigners say the environment is taking a beating at the hands of these Full Monty-style ladyboys. Several complaints have been lodged with the district council concerning a buildup of discarded sequinned dresses at the shoreline, and size eleven stilettos have washed up on beaches as far away as Bournemouth.

Todd says the beach needs to be shut down before an accident waits to happen.

"It won't be long before normal, law abiding nudists like myself can't bring a cub scout volleyball team down for an innocent day on the beach without being forced to watch grown men not dressed as women," he told reporters, blushing all over.

ROGER MELLIE THE MAN ON THE TELLY

FARMER PALMER

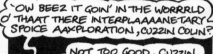

SUICIDAL SYD

He's always trying to pop his cork!

MY TELLY HAS BEEN BROKEN FOR THREE YEARS AND I'VE JUST GOT IT FIXED. I'M REALLY LOOKING FORWARD TO THIS REALITY TV EVERYONE IS TALKING ABOUT.

JESUS! IT'S A LIVE WEBCAM OF MAUREEN REES OFF DRIVING SCHOOL WIPING HER ARSE.

I THINK THE GRAVE IS PREFERABLE TO THAT!

AHA! SUFFRAGETTE EMILY WILDING DAVISON THREW HERSELF BENEATH THE HOOVES OF THE KING'S HORSE AT THE 1913 EPSOM DERBY!

WHAT A WAY TO GO!

LIBRARY

SUCCESSFUL SUICIDES OF HISTORY

I'LL DO LIKEWISE. AH, HERE COMES A FINE STEED RIGHT NOW.

EH? WHAT'S GOING ON?

SORRY, SYD. I'VE PULLED UP WITH A FURLONG TO GO AS PART OF AN INTERNET BETTING SCAM.

GLOOM

BAH! THAT DOESN'T IMPROVE MY FAITH IN HUMAN NATURE.

I'VE COME TO AMERICA TO BREAK INTO CHARLTON HESTON'S GARDEN.

NO TO GUNS

WHEN HE SEES ME WITH THIS SIGN, THE TRIGGER-HAPPY TWAT WILL BLAST ME TO KINGDOM COME.

WHAT IN GODDAMN IS GOIN' ON?

I'M A MEMBER OF THE ANTI-GUN LOBBY AND I'M TRESPASSING ON YOUR GARDEN YOU OLD COOT. YOU'D BETTER GET YOUR RIFLE AND "DAMN ME ALL TO HELL"!

SORRY SON, I CAN'T HEAR YOU. MY HEAD'S SHRUNK WITH AGE AND MY WIG'S SLIPPED OVER MY EARS.

WOULD IT INSPIRE YOU TO GUN ME DOWN IF I DRESSED UP AS A "DAMNED DIRTY APE"?

WHAT?

FORGET IT.

HERE I AM, THE NEXT DAY, BACK AT HOME ON MY COMPUTER, — AND I'M IN LUCK! I'VE MADE CONTACT WITH A GERMAN CANNIBAL ON THE INTERNET!

I'VE ARRANGED A MEETING. HEE HEE! TEN MINUTES WITH HIM AND MY ARSE IS SAUSAGES.

BAH! IT'S A PRE-PUBESCENT SCHOOLGIRL POSING AS A GERMAN CANNIBAL. JUST MY LUCK!

A RIGHT-WING CHRISTIAN FUNDAMENTALIST GROUP HAS BLOCK-BOOKED THE CINEMA TO WATCH THE PASSION OF CHRIST.

FULCHESTER MULTIPLEX

THE PASSION OF CHRIST

THEY'LL BE TURNING OUT SOON AND THEY'LL RIP ME TO PIECES!

OPEN THEM GATES. I'M A COMING THROUGH!

YES, IT'S TRUE, WE WERE FURIOUS AT THE BIT WHEN YOU JEWS KILLED OUR LORD, BUT WE WERE ALSO MOVED BY THE FILM'S PORTRAYAL OF CHRIST'S MESSAGE OF BROTHERLY LOVE.

HOW MOVING. IN FACT, THE CHRISTIAN MESSAGE HAS TOUCHED MY HEART.

I THINK I'LL GO FOR A NICE WALK IN THE COUNTRY TO APPRECIATE GOD'S BEAUTY.

I'LL POP IN HERE AND BID A CHEERY CHRISTIAN HELLO TO THE FARMER.

HMM. THERE'S NO ANSWER. I'LL JUST CLIMB IN THROUGH THE KITCHEN WINDOW TO SEE IF ANYONE'S IN.

KNOCK KNOCK

HELLO? HEL-

BLAM! BLAM!

TONY MARTIN, FARMER

GPO/LEW STRINGER VIZ 134

OUTCAST of the PONY BALLET SCHOOL

EASTENDERS HARDCASE PHIL MITCHELL ALIAS ACTOR STEVE MCFADDEN WAS STARTING HIS FIRST DAY AS A NEW PUPIL AT ST MARTHA'S SCHOOL OF PONY BALLET IN SUSSEX.

THE HEADMISTRESS WAS MISS SHARPE

AH, YOU'LL BE OUR NEW PUPIL. MCFADDEN, ISN'T IT?

TAKE YOUR PONY AND BALLET COSTUME OVER TO THE GYM — IT'S TIME FOR FIRST LESSON.

IN THE CHANGING ROOM THE OTHER GIRLS WERE DISCUSSING THEIR PARENTS' AGAS.

WELL WE USED TO HAVE A RAYBURN BUT NOW WE'VE GOT A 4-OVEN AGA WITH THE CERAMIC OPTION ON THE WARMING PLATE.

WE'VE GOT THE 2-OVEN MODEL IN PISTACHIO.

YOU'RE NEW HERE, AREN'T YOU? WHAT SORT OF AGA DOES YOUR FAMILY HAVE?

I-I'M FROM THE EAST END OF LONDON. WE DON'T HAVE AGAS THERE.

A GIRL NAMED VICTORIA SNEERED AT STEVE'S REPLY

UGH! THE EAST END OF LONDON! HOW DREADFULLY COMMON!

THE STANDARDS OF THIS SCHOOL MUST BE SLIPPING IF THE LOWER CLASSES ARE BEING ALLOWED IN.

COME ALONG GIRLS, THAT'S ENOUGH CHATTER

WE'VE GOT A LOT OF PONY BALLET TO PRACTISE

MISS SHARPE TOOK THE CLASS THROUGH THEIR PACES

ONE TWO THREE AND KICK TWO THREE

COME ON, PICK THOSE HOOVES UP

REALLY MCFADDEN, THAT SCRUFFY PONY OF YOURS IS SO GRACELESS

WHERE ON EARTH DID YOU GET IT FROM? AN EAST END RAG AND BONE YARD?

BURNING WITH RAGE, STEVE GRABBED AT VICTORIA'S HAIR

DON'T YOU DARE SAY A WORD AGAINST MY CHESTNUT!

OH! MISS SHARPE, HELP!

SHE'S THE BEST PONY IN THE WHOLE WORLD!

I'M DISAPPOINTED IN YOU, MCFADDEN. YOU'LL HAVE TO CONTROL THAT PROLETARIAN TEMPER OF YOURS

YOU'D BETTER LEAVE THE CLASS UNTIL YOU HAVE CALMED DOWN.

OH DEAR, CHESTNUT. I FEAR THAT I SHALL NEVER BE ACCEPTED HERE

EVERYONE LOOKS DOWN ON ME BECAUSE OF MY COMMON BACKGROUND.

THAT EVENING IN THE DORMITORY

WHAT'S THIS, MCFADDEN? SOME KIND OF CHEAP WORKING CLASS NECKLACE?

PLEASE LEAVE THAT ALONE, VICTORIA. IT'S A FAMILY HEIRLOOM.

NONSENSE! COMMON FAMILIES LIKE YOURS DON'T HAVE HEIRLOOMS. I EXPECT YOU BOUGHT IT FROM WOOLWORTHS.

THERE! I'VE THROWN IT OUT OF THE WINDOW

NO!

STEVE LEAPT ONTO CHESTNUT AND RACED AFTER THE NECKLACE

QUICK, CHESTNUT - WE'VE GOT TO FIND THAT NECKLACE!

OH! MISS SHARPE!

MCFADDEN! WHAT PLEBIAN TOMFOOLERY ARE YOU ENGAGED IN NOW?

I-I'M SORRY MISS SHARPE. BUT I SIMPLY HAD TO GET MY NECKLACE BACK — YOU SEE, IT BELONGED TO MY GREAT-GREAT GRANDMOTHER

WHAT? BUT THIS IS EXTRAORDINARY!

MR ROGERS WAS THE HISTORY TEACHER AT ST MARTHA'S

YOU SEE THIS INSIGNIA ON THE BACK OF THE PENDANT? THAT IS THE ROYAL CREST OF THE EXOTIC FARAWAY COUNTRY OF ZOGLAVIA

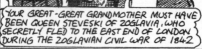

YOUR GREAT-GREAT GRANDMOTHER MUST HAVE BEEN QUEEN STEVESKI OF ZOGLAVIA, WHO SECRETLY FLED TO THE EAST END OF LONDON DURING THE ZOGLAVIAN CIVIL WAR OF 1842

STEVE'S MIND WAS IN A WHIRL

MY GREAT-GREAT GRANDMOTHER? A QUEEN?

BUT - BUT THAT MEANS I'M NOT FROM A COMMON BACKGROUND AFTER ALL

THAT IS CORRECT. AS HEIR TO THE ZOGLAVIAN THRONE, YOU ARE IN FACT A PRINCESS...

PRINCESS STEVE MCFADDEN OF ZOGLAVIA!

WHEN THE OTHER GIRLS HEARD OF STEVE'S ROYAL ANCESTRY, THEY TREATED HIM WITH A NEW RESPECT AND ACCEPTED HIM AS A FRIEND.

NEVER AGAIN WOULD STEVE MCFADDEN BE CALLED THE OUTCAST OF ST MARTHA'S PONY BALLET SCHOOL.

TONY SLATTERY & his PHONEY CATTERY

NO HOPE FOR POPE?

By The Joe Dolci Music Theatre

A tearaway pope has been banned from a shopping centre in Cumbria for persistent troublemaking – and if he shows no contrition then he could soon become the first pope to be served with an Anti-Social Behaviour Order.

84 year old John Paul II of Vatican City, Rome, continually harassed customers and staff at the Greendale Centre in Carlisle in a reign of terror lasting eighteen months. He is also thought to be the ringleader of the self-styled Infallible Gang whose members dress as bad cardinals and use abusive and dogmatic language.

issued

Police cautioned Mr II yesterday and issued him with the banning order on behalf of the shopping centre. The delinquent supreme pontiff admitted that he had used a magic marker to write "4 REAL" on an "I like the Pope, the Pope smokes dope" muscle top immediately prior to his arrest in Qwality Noveltys.

Greendale security staff confirmed the naughty pope had also ~

- *sprayed his graffiti tag 'PoJoPo' on several shopfronts*
- *stolen a public address system handset and broadcast Easter messages at shoppers anything up to four times a day*
- *consecrated sausage & egg McMuffins™ and chocolate milkshakes*
- *beatified confused HMV sales assistants*
- *posted dog muck through the returned video slot at Blockbuster*

bless you

John Paul II, who changed his name from Karol Wojtyla in 1978 to avoid a parking fine, may not return to the complex until such a time as he is offered absolution for his misdemeanours. His mother Beryl, 99, declined to be interviewed although she did express the view that her son's behaviour emphasized the problems faced by a single parent in modern society.

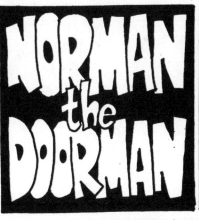

Letterbocks

Letterbocks, Viz Comic, PO Box 1PT, Newcastle upon Tyne NE99 1PT **Email: letters@viz.co.uk**

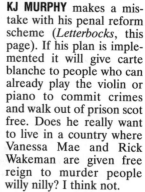

STAR LETTER

You often hear that "blood is thicker than water". Well I've got both of them coming out of my arse at the moment, and to be perfectly honest I can't feel any difference.

Ron Lilycropp, Email

PRINCE Charles recently complained that the education system encourages people to think they are qualified to do jobs which are beyond their abilities. I for one think we should listen to him as he clearly speaks with the voice of experience. Thanks to what I can only assume is a combination of bloody hard work and natural ability he has, since leaving school with 2 A-levels (a B in history and a C in French), gone to Cambridge University, become Duke of Cornwall and Rothesay, Earl of Chester, Baron Renfrew, a Wing Commander, a published author, an Air Commodore, Lord of the Isles and Great Steward of Scotland as well as being appointed Colonel in Chief of 9 regiments and a barrister. Not only that, he has been knighted three times (the first time at the age of

10) and was honoured with the Coronation Medal when he was a mere 5 years old. If only the rest of us could follow his shining example, the world would be a much better place.

Mrs S Embleton
Carshalton

Traveller's CRIME WATCH

TALK ABOUT *loudmouth wankers on public transport? I was unfortunate enough to encounter this suit-jacket/T-shirt/converse-wearing offender on the 01.05 London Waterloo to Winchester train late in the evening of Sunday 7th November. Although the target for his loudly projected voice was a bored looking girl sitting approximately two feet from his facking mouth, myself and other passengers were treated to a monologue which encompassed his family's university history, his pending career as a journalist or comedy* scriptwriter (undecided), *his amazing sporting prowess and his dazzling musical insight. Twat.*

Bill Beaumont,
e-mail

SHOULD any *Viz* readers wish to meet the rudest, most impolite, self-important tosspot imaginable, go to my local Post Office, third counter from the left. The ginger-bearded cunt there won't disappoint you.

Kevin Smith
Brindley Thorpe, York

IN MY local library there is a warning sign which reads 'There is a thief at work in this library'. I find it disgusting that the council expects me to fork out a fortune in rates each year to keep scum like this in employment.

P Snodgrass
Bury St Edmonds

MY BROTHER is a friend of beardy ex-Wizard frontman Roy Wood. Three years ago, on the evening of December 25th I accompanied him to a party at the singer's home. 'I wish it could be Christmas Every Day' shall forever henceforth sound bitterly ironic to me, since there were only seven guests there and we spent the evening bored, bollock cold, sitting round a gas fire sipping warm cans of Carling Black Label.

Nad Hamilton
Derby

"HISTORY has a habit of repeating itself" goes the old saying. I should say so! On the UKTV History channel, I've seen the same programme about Cleopatra about five times in the last couple of months.

Alan J Thackray
Email

ON *Ready Steady Cook* the contestants are given a budget of £5 to spend on ingredients. Several times now I've witnessed a contestant say they went over

the budget by a few pence, only for them to be allowed to carry on with the show completely unpunished. Come on Ainsley, these people are walking all over you. Lay down the fucking law, mate.

Alex Oliver
Email

AFTER a concert, Carol Decker out of T'Pau once famously returned to her dressing room to find her clothes spattered with semen. Although the culprit has never been found, I find it interesting that Cliff Richard has never explicitly denied being responsible.

As a Christian, if he swore on the bible that he had never ejaculated onto Ms Decker's clothing I would have no option but to accept that he was telling the truth. So why doesn't he clear the air? Something to hide, perhaps?

J Venturi
Carshalton

WHAT faith am I supposed to have in the 3 years parts & labour warranty on my new Mercedes-Benz? After all, their 'Thousand year Reich' lasted barely fifteen years.

CD Stomper
Thackbridge

I HAVE an idea which could revolutionise the penal system in Britain. If somebody has been convicted of murder or something they should be locked away in a room with, say, a piano or a violin and then told that they are not allowed out until they are really good. When the time comes for them to be released they will have served their time and will be able to make amends by doing high standard concerts in the Albert Hall.

KJ Murphy
Email

KJ MURPHY makes a mistake with his penal reform scheme (*Letterbocks*, this page). If his plan is implemented it will give carte blanche to people who can already play the violin or piano to commit crimes and walk out of prison scot free. Does he really want to live in a country where Vanessa Mae and Rick Wakeman are given free reign to murder people willy nilly? I think not.

F Bjornhansen
Guildford

THOSE who complain that too few people observe the two minutes' silence should blame the military planners. If they had stopped the war on the fifth hour of the fifth day of the fifth month then we would all observe the silence, because at 5am we would all be in bed.

Alan Guff
Email

IT'S all very well when the newsreaders remind us that our clocks have to go back, but I've got five clocks in my house and I can't remember where I bought them.

Jason Simmons
Email

WHEN someone zipped up Zippy's mouth zip on *Rainbow*, why did he always make such a brou-ha-ha about it? Why didn't he just unzip it himself and keep on talking?

KJ Murphy again
Warrington

"WHEN a man loves a woman, can't keep his mind on nuthin' else" crooned Percy Sledge during the summer of 1966. I would have to disagree, as during sexual intercourse with my wife I routinely think about our next door neighbour Brenda and her border collie.

David Thompson
Email

YEARS AGO my mother went to see Lance Percival perform in Margate, having promised my sister that she would obtain the noted comedy calypso artiste's autograph. She forgot but, rather enterprisingly, forged Mr Percival's name in my sister's autograph book upon returning home. Her deception was never discovered by my sister. Personally, I don't think anyone comes out of this looking too good.

Chris Blunkell
Email

BONO out of U2 sang "I still haven't found what I'm looking for". Maybe it would be easier to find if he took those bloody sunglasses off when he is indoors.

Kieran Murphy
Cheshire

IN DAYS of old, Knights of the Realm were chosen for their ability to fight bravely against fierce dragons or in wars against the Ottoman Empire etc. However, we'd be in a pretty pickle if we had to rely on modern knights like Sir Elton John, Sir Ian McKellan or Sir Frederick Ashton to save the country from a dangerous foe these days. Imagine that lot mincing up to the battle lines at Agincourt. We'd have been fucked before the battle even kicked off.

H Brookes-Baker
Epsom

IT'S A sobering thought that if Marilyn Monroe had lived, she would have been 78 years old now. At that age, though, I for one wouldn't fancy looking up her skirt when she walked over a grate, so it's probably just as well she's dead.

Mr Rice
Trowbridge

LAMES to FAME

The brother of Nigel who used to be in *EastEnders* was a patient at the hospital where my dad works. Keep it under your hats, though. It's confidential NHS information.

CM Lindsay, Email

My ex-wife's brother-in-law's mum's next-door neighbour is the brother of Les McKeown out of the Bay City Rollers. Or, if you will, Les McKeown out of the Bay City Rollers's brother lives next door to my sister-in-law's mother-in-law.

Jamie Bartleet, Hyde

I've got a friend whose driving instructor claims to be Peter Andre's uncle.

Mark Entwistle, Email

My uncle used to work for the gas board and he installed central heating for a guy who stayed two doors down from the woman who hung up the Krankies' panto costumes in their dressing room in Glasgow around 1986.

Dipper, Glasgow

Leo Sayer's mother-in-law once came to my mum's house for tea. He came to pick her up but the anti-social bastard just tooted the horn outside and wouldn't come in.

Aaliclar, Email

I got talking to a heating engineer who got called out to a problem at a cinema where I once worked. It transpired that he used to be an undertaker who specialised in the repatriation of people who had died whilst overseas. He told me he'd screwed the lid on Kirsty McColl and Worzel Gummidge actor Jon Pertwee when they were sent back to England, and he also posted Please Sir's Derek Guyler off to Australia when he kicked the bucket.

Muvals Cunit, Email

My dad could have bought a Rover previously owned by *Coronation Street's* Elsie Tanner.

Looks like FainfA%
Stockport

I occasionally have a drink with a bloke who has shagged the actress who plays La-La the Tellytubby. The yellow one.

MJ Smith, Email

I shared a bed with Cilla Black in Somerset. Not at the same time, though. She had apparently stayed at the same hotel some time before. Or it might have been my brother as we are not sure which of the twin beds she had slept in.

Julian Miller (or my brother Bill)
Email

Mark King, ape-faced mega thumb-tastic Level 42 bass player, lives (or maybe not now, but definitely lived) on the Isle of Wight, next door to a bloke at work's ex-missus's grandparents, and their dog bit him on the chin.

Dave, Email

TOP TIPS

MEN. When listening to your favourite CD, simply turn up the sound to the volume you desire; then turn it down three notches. This will save your wife from having to do it.

Paul Hargreaves, e-mail

MARK LAWRENSON. When the camera moves away from you in a wide shot on Football Focus, don't do that shifty sideways glance to see if you are still on screen as you get caught every time.

Mark Bates, e-mail

DON'T waste money on expensive ipods. Simply think of your favourite tune and hum it. If you want to "switch tracks", simply think of another song you like and hum that instead.

Fish Kid, Email

HEALTH SERVICE managers. Save millions by replacing the costly 'NHS Direct' service with a simple recorded message that says, "It's probably OK, but if it doesn't start getting better, pop along to Accident and Emergency."

Martin W, London

WOMEN. Don't waste energy faking orgasms. Most men couldn't give a shit anyway and you could use the saved energy to hoover the house after you've been banged.

Lee Cawood, Hull

PET OWNERS. Rats make ideal 'large print' mice for short-sighted cats.

Matthew Phillimore, e-mail

SPOOK owners of cars with tinted windows. Upon seeing one driving past, wink conspiratorially and touch your nose.

Ed Wullbeck, e-mail

THAT's How Rich I Am!

~A series of profiles in which tawdry celebrities boast about the extent of their wealth.

No. 23
Noel Edmonds

*"I've got an automatic tennis ball serving machine. However, I don't use it for tennis, I simply fill it full of tennis-ball sized diamonds and fire them into a lake, 24 hours a day. **That's** how rich I am."*

Next week: Cilla Black~ *"I wipe my arse on Rembrandts."*

Our Walnut's a Teacher

DO YOU FANCY ANYTHING FROM THE KITCHEN, DEAR?

OOH, YES PLEASE. I'D LIKE A NUT.

WHAT SORT WOULD YOU PREFER...A BRAZIL NUT, A PECAN NUT, A PISTACCHIO NUT..?

ERM... A WALNUT PLEASE, DEAR.

OH, LORDY! IT'S THE **FAT SLAGS...**

HEY, 'AVE Y' SEEN THE SUN?... THEY'VE CAUGHT DIRTY DEN 'AVIN' **WEB SEX**... EURGH!

DIRTY LITTLE BASTARD. FANCY LETTIN' ALL SPIDERS RUN OVER YER COCK FORRA THRILL

NO, Y' DAFT COW, IT'S NOWT T' DO WI' SPIDERS. IT'S THE INTERWEB... Y' KNOW... COMPUTER SEX

OH

DIRTY LITTLE BASTARD. FANCY STICKIN' YER COCK IN YER COMPUTER FORRA THRILL

IT'S A WONDER HE WEREN'T FUCKIN' **ELECTROCUTED!**

NO... NO... SAN... NO... THAT'S NOT WEB SEX. WEB SEX IS... Y' KNOW... **VIRTUAL** INTERCOURSE

WHAT?... LIKE WHEN DAVE'S 'AD A SKINFUL AN' HE CAN'T QUITE THUMB IT ALL THE WAY IN?

NO... WEB SEX IS A VERY EROTIC, BEAUTIFUL AN' SENSUAL THING...

Y' LINK UP WI' SOME BIRD ON A WEB CAM, THEN Y' WRITE DIRTY MESSAGES AN' WATCH EACH OTHER PULLIN' YER-SELVES OFF

'OW D' **YOU** KNOW? YEAH?

I KNOW, LADIES... BECAUSE I AM, DIRK DIAMONDCUTTER, AN' I HAVE WEB SEX ALL THE FUCKIN' TIME.

DIRK DIAMONDCUTTER?

WELL, DIRK DIAMONDCUTTER 712, ACTUALLY. IT'S ME **LOG-ON** NAME... LAST NIGHT, I WAS CYBER BANGIN' JUICY LUCY 363 IN SYDNEY

'OO'S SHE?

FUCK KNOWS! THAT'S THE SEXY THING ABOUT IT, SEE... IT'S ALL TOTALLY ANONYMOUS

WELL, I'M DEAD JEALOUS... YOU 'AVIN' WEB SEX WI' SOMEBODY IS LIKE CHEATIN' ON ME

AYE!... AN' WHAT ABOUT YER MISSUS?

DOES **SHE** KNOW Y' SIT THERE WI' A LOG-ON WATCHIN' SOME AUSSIE FLICKIN' 'ER BEAN?

WHAT?... SHE'D 'AVE ME KNACKERS ON A FUCKIN' PLATE....

...NAH! THE COMPUTER'S IN THE BOX ROOM... SHE THINKS I'M PLAYIN' ON ME FLIGHT SIMULATOR... SAT THERE WI' ME JOYSTICK IN ME HAND

WELL, SHE'S HALF RIGHT, THEN

WELL, I SAY IF YER GOIN' TO 'AVE WEB SEX WI' SOMEBODY, IT OUGHT T' BE WI' **ME**, BAZ...

... COME ON, TRAY

SO... COME ON, LET'S GET 'OME AN' SET THIS LOT UP... I'M CHOKIN' FORRA BIT O' WEB SEX

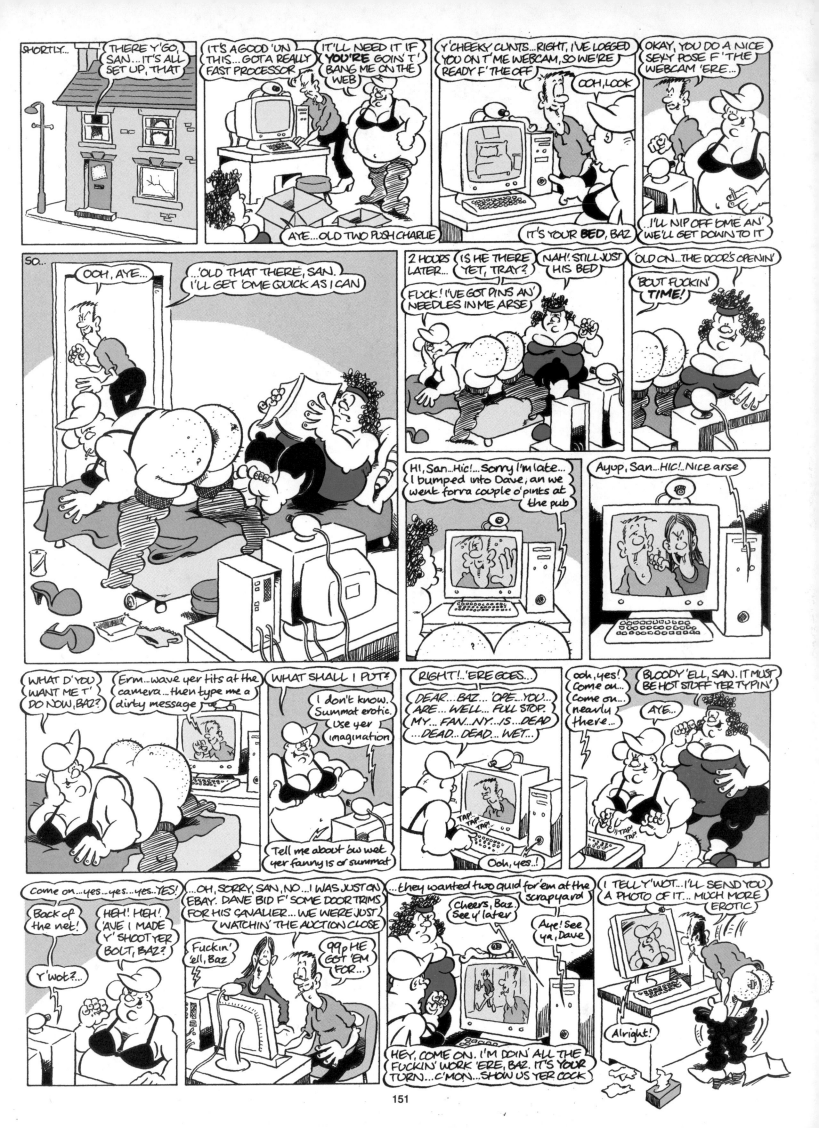

151

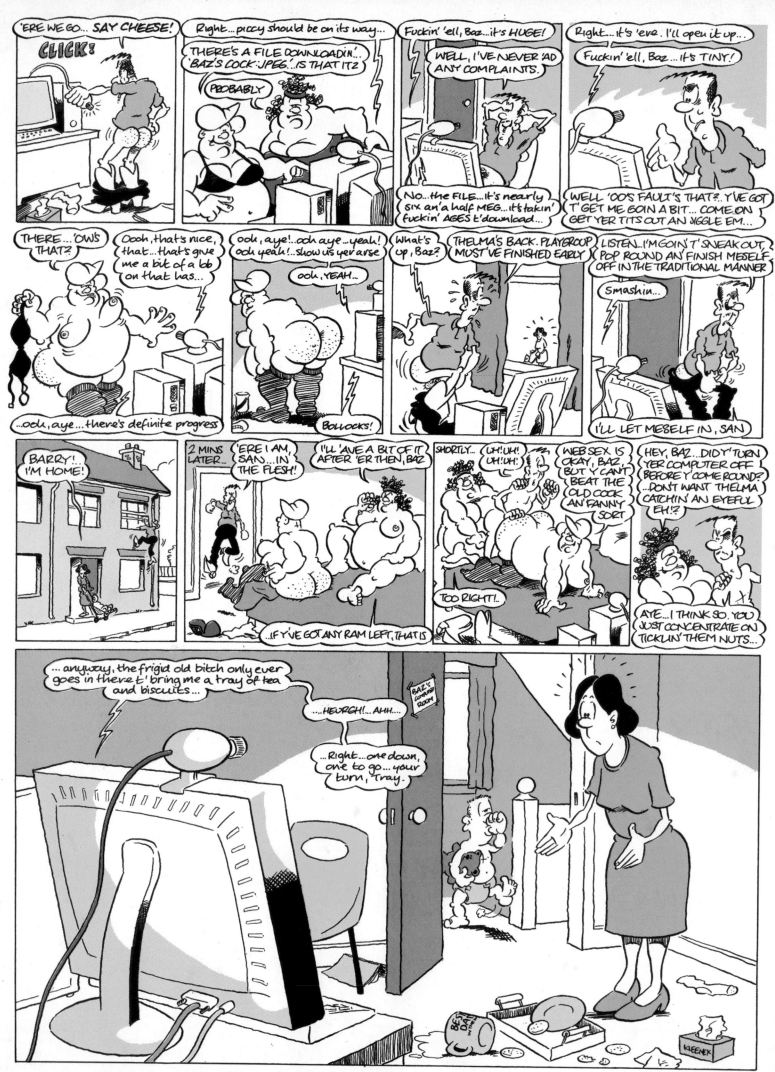

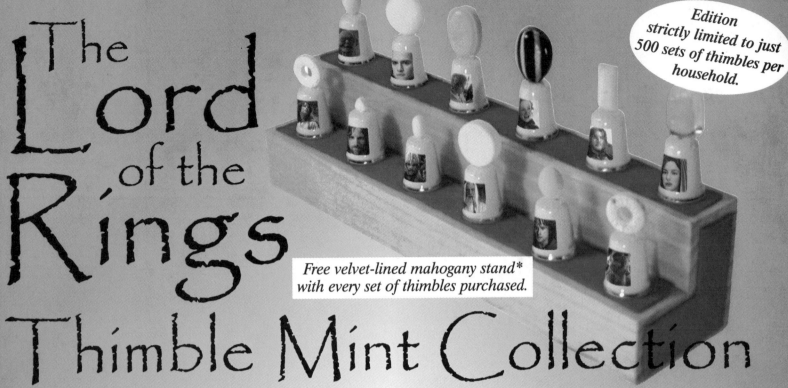

CHRISTMAS with the BACONS

CHRISTMAS DAY
HOY, BIFFA! THE QUEEN'S SPEECH IS ON THE TELLY

REET, FATHA. I'M COMIN' NOO.

IT HAS BEEN A CANNY GOOD YEAR THROUGHOOT THE HURL FUCKIN' COMMONWEALTH, AN' I WISH A MERRY CHRISSMUS TO AALL MY SUBJECTS...

...AALL EXCEPT BIFFA, WHO IS A REET LIRREL CUNT AND DESORVES TO GET HIS FUCKIN' HEED KICKED IN

Y'HEAR THAT, BIFFA? THAT WAS A ROYAL COMMAND TELLIN' US TO KICK YOUR HEED IN

HAD ON, FATHA, HAD ON! THAT WAS NEVER THE REAL QUEEN'S SPEECH...

...IT'S JUST MUTHA WEARING A PAPER CROON AN' SITTIN' INSIDE AN URLD TELLY CABINET

YEE MUST THINK A'M FUCKIN' DAFT, YEE

SHORTLY
...AND FINALLY I WOULD LIKE TO EXTEND MY WARMEST REGARDS TO ALL OF MY SUBJECTS THROUGHOUT THE COMMONWEALTH

A VERY HAPPY CHRISTMAS, AND A PROSPEROUS NEW YEAR TO YOU ALL...

...ALL EXCEPT BIFFA, WHO IS A RIGHT LITTLE CUNT AND DESERVES TO GET HIS FUCKING HEAD KICKED IN

HEH HEH! REET!

GULP!

Captain Morgan AND HIS HAMMOND ORGAN

'TIS TRUE, ME CUT-THROAT HEARTIES! THAT ISLAND HAS A KING'S RANSOM IN SPANISH DOUBLOONS, JUST WAITING TO BE PLUNDERED!

THIS HERE MAP WILL DIRECT YE TO THE TREASURE. GO HENCE, AND FILL YER POCKETS WITH PIECES OF EIGHT!

ARE YE NOT COMING WITH US TO THE ISLAND, CAP'N?

NO, MATEYS. I MUST...ERM... REMAIN ON BOARD TO KEEP WATCH FOR THE BRITISH NAVY.

SOME TIME LATER
SHIVER ME TIMBERS! SEVEN HOURS OF DIGGING, AND NOT A SIGN OF THE TREASURE!

BUT WHY WOULD THE CAP'N SEND US ON A WILD GOOSE CHASE?

MERRY CHRISTMAS

THE JOLLY BLUE BARNACLE GRAND XMAS PARTY

SURPRISE!

WHAT IN THE BLUE BLAZES?!

HA-HARR! I THOUGHT YE'D APPRECIATE MY LITTLE CHRISTMAS TREAT, SHIPMATES. NOW LET'S GET THE PARTY SWINGING WITH A MEDLEY OF RESTIVE FAVOURITES ON MY HAMMOND TONEWHEEL B3 ORGAN

HERE'S ONE TO GET US ALL IN A SEASONAL MOOD...

FROS-TY THE SNOWMAN WAS A JOL-LY HAPPY SOUL

WITH A CORNCOB PIPE AND A BUTTON NOSE AND TWO EYES MADE OF COAL

OR HOW ABOUT THIS ONE...
COME THEY TOLD ME, PARUMPA-PUM-PUM A NEW BORN KING TO SEE, PARUMPA PUM PUM

YOU'RE COMIN' WITH US, CAP'N

AYE. AND YER ACCURSED HAMMOND ORGAN

OUR FINEST GIFTS WE BRING, PARUMPA-PUM-PUM TO LAY BEFORE THE KING PARUMPA-PUM-PUM

RUMPA-PUM-PUM

RUMPA-PUM-PUM

THAT'S ENOUGH, CAP'N. WE'RE GOING TO KEEL-HAUL YOU UNDER THE SHIP

WAIT, YE SCURVY SWABS! AFORE YE CAST ME INTO THE BRINY BLUE, STOP A MOMENT AND THINK!

...THINK OF THOSE LESS FORTUNATE LUBBERS WHO WON'T BE HAVING A MERRY CHRISTMAS THIS YEAR...

IT'S CHRISTMASTIME THERE'S NO NEED TO FEEL...

GLUB!

SPLOSH

HEAVE-HO! HEAVE-HO! HEAVE-HO!

HA-HARR! THE CAP'N WILL BE TORN TO SHREDS AS HE'S DRAGGED UNDER THE SHIP

HEAVE-HO!

HERE HE COMES NOW, MATES!

GLOOP GLUB BLUBBLE BLOIK

...DO THEY KNOW IT'S CHRISS-MUS TIME AT ALL?

FEED THE WUR-UR-URLD

SPOILT BASTARD

THE LADS FROM BUSTED: Charlie (middle) and Matt (right).

As chart-topping boyband Busted complete their record-breaking nationwide sellout tour, we meet Charlie, Matt and Ken to give them a grilling about life, love and music.

You've just completed a sellout nationwide tour, filling stadiums from one end of the country to the other. Does life on the road sometimes get a bit dull?

Matt: Yeah, it can do. But we're always getting up to loony pranks to keep ourselves entertained.

Charlie: Yeah, like the time we went into our support band McFly's hotel room and lit a fire in the wastepaper bin!

Ken: There was smoke everywhere. The sprinklers went off and they had to evacuate the whole building. It was absolutely mental!

Bands get up to all sorts of tricks to relieve the boredom of touring. What sort of high jinks have you got up to?

Ken: All sorts. We're absolutely mad!

Charlie: Once on the tour bus, Matt got out these supersoakers which he'd filled with petrol.

Ken: Matt was like, let's have a competition to see who can burn the driver's hat off!

Matt: Yeah, it was mad! Charlie went first and totally missed. The driver lost all the skin off the back of his head and his neck. It looked so funny!

Charlie: We all just cracked up.

How do you relieve the boredom of life on tour?

Charlie: We play a lot of practical jokes on our crew. There was this one roadie who was always playing tricks on us, like hiding our guitars and putting them out of tune when we weren't looking.

Matt: Yeah. We thought we'd get our own back on him. So one night after a gig, the three of us burst into his room, gagged him and tied him to his bed with gaffer tape.

Ken: Then we set fire to his mattress and locked the door!

Matt: We absolutely p*ssed ourselves!

Travelling between gigs must get pretty boring from time to time. What do you do to break the monotony?

Ken: All sorts. This one time we were on tour and having some pub-licity photos taken at some zoo. God, it was SO boring!

Charlie: I thought I'd liven things up a bit, so I doused one of the gibbons with lighter fuel and set it on fire!

Matt: It was hilarious! You've never seen a monkey move so fast. It was swinging through the cage making these funny whooping sounds and setting all the other apes on fire as it went past.

Charlie: Yeah. In the end the whole cage was full of burning monkeys leaping about making these stupid noises! We p*ssed ourselves!

Ken: You should have seen the keeper's face! It was a picture!

Life on the road must get dull from time to time. How do you keep yourselves entertained?

Matt: Touring can be dull, but we do have lots of fun. For example, our manager's a real square, and we love winding him up.

Charlie: This one time, we were on CD:UK and Matt was like, let's flush his phone down the toilet!

Matt: He was so mad! He marched straight into our dressing room to b*ll*ck us, but Ken was hiding behind the door with a tyre full of petrol!

Ken: I put it round his neck and lit it! He totally went up like a rocket!

Matt: It was so funny! We were laughing about it so much when we went on the show we couldn't even play our guitars.

Charlie: Or sing.

SELL-OUT: Some of the sold out tickets from the boys' recent sell-out nationwide tour.

GREAT SCOTTISH FOOTBALLING MOMENTS

AW SHITE MAN!

© G. TW 2004

A-Z of Jonny W

IN THE DYING SECONDS of the rugby World Cup final, superstar Jonny Wilkinson kicked his way into the annals of sporting history. With his unerring left foot he single-handedly brought the coveted William Webb-Ellis trophy back to Britain, whilst with his scrummy good looks he brought the nation's women to its knees.

THE whole nation has gone *Jonny crazy*. It's like Beatlemania all over again, but with Jonny Wilkinson instead of the Beatles.

We know about the public figure, but how much do we know about the private man behind the mask. Here's a comprehensive **A-Z** of the man who made Britain Great again.

A is for Ant.
You might think that Jonny's fantastic kick in the dying seconds of the World Cup final would be the most thrilling moment of his life... *but you'd be wrong*. On Radio 4's *Desert Island Discs* programme he told Sue Lawley that the highlight of his life so far was meeting his childhood hero Ant out of Ant and Dec.

B is for Buttocks.
When he was twelve, Johnny developed a skin-rash on his posterior. It was so unusual that a consultant asked him if he'd mind showing his bottom during one of his lectures at a medical school. This early experience of dropping his trousers and showing his arse to a roomful of students led him to take up rugby in later life. *The rest is history!*

C is for Cheese.
Jonny doesn't have a favourite cheese. He thinks they're all equally delicious, especially Stilton.

D is for Dec
You might think that skidding off the A1 and hitting a tree at Leeming Bar would be the low point of Jonny's life... *but you'd be wrong.*

On Radio 4's *Moral Maze* programme he told Michael Buerk that it had been the time he met his least favourite kids' TV presenter, Dec out of Ant and Dec.

E is for Elephants.
Like the mother of Victorian 'Elephant Man' Jonny Merrick, Jonny Wilkinson's mother was trampled by a circus elephant whilst pregnant. However, there the similarity ends. For Wilkinson turned into a handsome rugby hero whose kick in the dying seconds won the World Cup for England, whilst Merrick grew into a blasphemous abomination of nature in a big cap.

F is for Falcons.
Few people realise that Jonny doesn't just play for England. He also occasionally turns out for Newcastle United's rugby team, Newcastle Falcons United.

G is for Gimp.
For several years Jonny has been in a steady relationship, so it's likely that his sexual tastes are probably fairly mainstream. It's unlikely that he ever gets his kicks by donning a tightly-fitting rubber gimp mask and strapping a ball into his mouth whilst a woman in a Gestapo uniform treads on his genitals with spiky stiletto shoes.

H is for History Books.
Jonny's heroic kick in the dying seconds of the world cup meant that the history books had to be re-written. It is estimated that publishers were forced to pulp over six million volumes of history on the Sunday following the match, whilst libraries throughout the world built huge bonfires of out-of-date history books. Leading historian Eric Hobsbawn has been working round the clock ever since to rewrite his history of the English Civil War to incorporate Jonny's thrilling achievement.

I is for Igloo.
Jonny lives in a large house in Northumberland. However, if he were an eskimo living at the North Pole, he would probably make his home in an igloo - a hemispherical snow dwelling with a tunnel entrance.

J is for Jam.
When he's not playing rugby, crashing his car or meeting the Queen, Jonny likes nothing more than tucking into his favourite food - jam sandwiches. However, he doesn't like bread, so he eats it straight from the jar... *with his fingers!*

K is for Kick.
Jonny spends 12 hours every day practising kicking balls in his garden. However his next door neighbour Mr Taylor refuses to give them back and is so fed up with them coming over the fence that he bursts them all... *approximately 50,000 rugby balls each year!*

L is for Las Vegas.
With lucrative advertising deals, endorsements and a hefty salary, Jonny is one of the richest men in sport. So rich, in fact, that if he travelled to Las Vegas and bet the lot on a single spin of a roulette wheel, he could win *thirty-two times his stake!* But it's not all good news - if his number didn't come up, *he could lose the lot!*

M is for Mary.
Whilst at nursery school Jonny was cast as a shepherd in the nativity play. On the day of the performance, the little girl who was set to play Mary fell ill with chicken pox, and Jonny was forced to step into the breach. This early experience of cross-dressing led him to take up rugby later in life. *The rest is history!*

N is for Nipples.
Jonny suffers from a rare medical condition called octopapillacy, which means he has an incredible 8 nipples, like a sow. His cruel schoolmates nicknamed him "Jonny Eight-tits", but he had the last laugh 20 years later, when his make or break kick in the dying seconds of the final secured the rugby World Cup trophy for England.

O is for OBE.
The Queen was so thrilled by Jonny's kick in the last few

Oh Jonny, oh Jonny, Oh... B... E - Hero Wilkinson prepares to take the last minute kick in the dying seconds of the rugby World Cup final which secured the trophy for England. Hurrah!